✒ Endorsements ✒

"Bold and breathtaking. Sweeping but sweet. Passionate yet practical. A vision of the magnitude of God's Son and the joy of our relationship to Him unlike anything I've ever read. When I set it down I truly felt I had been in a "Holy Presence." If I were to summarize this book with one phrase it would be: "intimacy with Christ's supremacy." I've watched Nancy Wilson live-out this truth for over twenty years. She's convinced me that this is God's destiny for every Christian. In some ways I feel there are no words adequate to express the true depth and impact of this book. Nancy's vision of the King is simply breathtaking, in the truest sense of that term."

-David Bryant, *author of CHRIST IS ALL! A Joyful Manifesto on the Supremacy of God's Son*

"The King of the Kingdom is coming to this planet to rule and reign with His Bride at His side. He has sent forerunners into the earth preparing the way of His coming. The passionate King is calling His promised Bride to rise and dance with Him to the Love Song of the Ages. The book and CD *The King and I* are arrows that hit the mark. Joyfully, read, listen and fall deeper in love with Jesus, our Bridegroom King."

-Mike Bickle, *author of After God's Own Heart and Passion for Jesus*

"Nancy shares her sweet communion and intimate fellowship with the King of kings. She gives us a beautiful picture of what it would be like if we also choose to allow God to romance our hearts and minds with His all-consuming love. If you so choose - your heart will never be the same."

-Fern Nichols, *President/Founder*
Moms In Touch International

D0916212

"We have known Nancy for many years and have always admired her deep love for her Lord, her zeal for life, and her passion to help win the world for Christ. Her work as Associate Director of Student Venture has provided her the opportunity to win thousands of high school students to Christ and help instill an enthusiasm to win their campuses for Christ as well. Nancy has deep compassion for the nations of the world. One of her greatest pleasures is to help people of every culture to know the love and forgiveness of God. Her personal and intimate walk with God is contagious. Everywhere she goes she radiates the love of God and is truly a light for Him."

-Steve and Judy Douglass
Campus Crusade for Christ International

"Old Testament saints generally approached God as His "unworthy servants." Because of Christ's sacrifice at Calvary He invites us to approach Him as His "made-worthy Bride." Nancy's 'The King and I' brings this truth into focus and provides us with practical application. Read it and be drawn "Beyond the Veil" with Him!"

-Alice Smith, author of **Beyond the Veil**
U.S. Prayer Center

"Nancy Wilson is a beautiful woman who has chosen in this life to give her love exclusively to the Lord Jesus. She is an amazing example of pure devotion to her Beloved who just happens to be the Creator and Savior of the Universe. I love the refreshing purity of this book-- and the beautiful reality it underscores that there is one "happily ever after" story that is true--the love story of Jesus and His followers. Even us guys can excited about that!

-Ron Boehme
Youth With A Mission

The
King and I

An Intimate Love Song to the Nations

ABOUT THE COVER:

The bride of Christ so taken in beauty of the bridegroom's eyes that in total surrender, she moves everywhere he gently leads. Together they dance across the earth in grace and beauty. Where their footsteps touch, the revival fire of their love spreads throughout the nations of the earth.

BY NANCY M. WILSON

Cover art by James Nesbit
Illustrations by Kae Mentz
Edited by Becky Hill
Worship CD produced by Steve Bell

The King and I: An Intimate Love Song to the Nations

Published by NewLife Publications
A ministry of Campus Crusade for Christ
P.O. Box 620877
Orlando, FL 32862-0877

Cover by James Nesbit
Edited by Becky Hill

Printed in the United States of America

ISBN 1-56399-251-5

"…Great and marvelous are your deeds,
Lord God Almighty.
Just and true are your ways,
KING OF THE AGES.
Who will not fear you, O Lord,
and bring glory to your name?
For you alone are holy.
All nations will come
and worship before you,
for your righteous acts have been revealed."
Revelation 15:3-4 (emphasis mine)

Contents

The
King and I
An Intimate Love Song to the Nations

Dedication

To my Prince and King, **Jesus**, my Savior, Lord and Lover of my soul. To You my heart belongs. To You my soul adores. To You I give my all. To You I offer this book, praying it will bring You the glory due You, calling forth Your Bride as we await Your return. For You are a great King and Your name is to be feared among the nations (Malachi 1:14).

Also to **Bill Bright**, whom I consider a spiritual father. As founder of Campus Crusade for Christ, he modeled and taught a life of supreme love and devotion to Jesus. "First Love for Jesus" was the cry of his heart. "Remember your leaders, who spoke the word of God to you. Consider the outcome of their way of life and imitate their faith" (Hebrews 13:7). I will be forever grateful to this beloved, humble servant and slave of Jesus for his loving influence in my life. His spiritual legacy extends to the farthest corners of the world. Truly he fulfilled the call of the Bride. "The spirit and the bride say, 'Come!'…" (Revelation 22:17).

Foreword

As I have read Nancy's book, *The King and I*, my heart has been moved time and time again. Had my precious husband, Bill, been reading it, he would have shed tears with almost every page. I've shed a few myself. I have never known anyone other than Bill's mother and Nancy who has had a greater love or a softer heart for the majesty of Jesus. It is appropriate that Nancy be the one to write this book and dedicate it to Bill Bright. She not only shares the passion of her heart, but that of others who know Christ so intimately.

The love of our great God and Savior has been a driving motivation in my life as well. Bill and I signed a contract many years ago to become slaves of Jesus, surrendering our lives to Him. Since then, He has shown us His intimate love in so many ways. Bill's passion and mine is first love for Jesus, the One who gave all for us on the cross. We have seen the heart of Jesus revealed all over the world in answer to prayer.

My desire and prayer is that the body of Christ would embrace the awesome truth that the King of the universe has come to earth to purchase His beloved Bride, the Church. In *The King and I*, Nancy brings us to a fresh realization of our glorious King, His beloved Bride, the Church, and the kingdom that is the fruit of this intimate partnership. Nancy beautifully lives out this message and her passion is contagious. I had the joy and privilege of being the bride of Bill Bright for 54 years, but nothing on this earth will ever be able to compare with being called the "Bride of Christ," now and throughout eternity.

I highly recommend *The King and I*. You will be captured by Christ's passionate love for you and inspired to pursue Him in a deeper way than ever before. The King is waiting to escort you on this journey. Nancy will be an inspiring and delightful guide.

Lovingly,

Vonette Z. Bright

Introduction

Much of the world watched with wide eyes as Prince Charles married Princess Diana in England. It was a real-life fairy tale.

Diana had been brought into the royal family simply by agreeing to marry the prince. A life of honor and excitement lay before her. And a small part of us, just a glimmer of hope, wished that someday a prince might come for us too. That we would be part of a royal kingdom, and live a life of honor.

But then their story ended in tragedy. The couple divorced after 15 years of marriage, and Diana died in a car accident a year after that. The fairy tale had been destroyed. And we lost hope.

The small, unspoken dream we had that one day we would be part of a royal kingdom, like Diana, died with her. The reality of life came crashing down. There would no fairy tale ending.

But there is a larger truth that we dare not miss. The story is not over yet. We are still waiting for the ultimate ending. We are part of a love story much greater than Charles and Diana, greater than any king and queen. We have a vital role in the greatest story ever told. It was born in the heart of our Creator, the King of the Universe. Jesus Christ has rescued us and redeemed us, and He calls us to join Him on a great adventure. More than that, He calls the Church to be His holy Bride.

But have we have fallen short of the call? Even if we call Christ "King" with our lips, do we really understand what it means to experience His royalty in our lives? We have lost our focus on building His eternal Kingdom, we have forgotten His heart to bring more people into a relationship with Him.

It is my prayer that the following chapters will renew the love story for you. That God would romance you and make you fall in love with Him again. That you would take up your role as His Bride with new enthusiasm, and seek hard after those He still wants in His Kingdom.

Join me as we see this intimate love story unfold, through Psalm 45, as it illustrates the way God pursues us. It is a wedding song, and the bride is a foreign princess. We too have been foreigners to God, but now He invites us, the Church, to be His royal Bride. Take a minute to read the psalm now, and notice the kind of words it uses to describe the king and his new bride.

Psalm 45

My heart is stirred by a noble theme
as I recite my verses for the king;
my tongue is the pen of a skillful writer.
You are the most excellent of men
and your lips have been anointed with grace,
since God has blessed you forever.
Gird your sword upon your side, O mighty one;
clothe yourself with splendor and majesty.
In your majesty ride forth victoriously
in behalf of truth, humility and righteousness;
let your right hand display awesome deeds.
Let your sharp arrows pierce the hearts of the king's enemies;
let the nations fall beneath your feet.
Your throne, O God, will last for ever and ever;
a scepter of justice will be the scepter of your kingdom.
You love righteousness and hate wickedness;
therefore God, your God, has set you above your companions
by anointing you with the oil of joy.
All your robes are fragrant with myrrh and aloes and cassia;
from palaces adorned with ivory
the music of the strings makes you glad.
Daughters of kings are among your honored women;
at your right hand is the royal bride in gold of Ophir.
Listen, O daughter, consider and give ear:
Forget your people and your father's house.

The king is enthralled by your beauty;
honor him, for he is your lord.
The Daughter of Tyre will come with a gift,
men of wealth will seek your favor.
All glorious is the princess within her chamber;
her gown is interwoven with gold.
In embroidered garments she is led to the king;
her virgin companions follow her
and are brought to you.
They are led in with joy and gladness;
they enter the palace of the king.
Your sons will take the place of your fathers;
you will make them princes throughout the land.
I will perpetuate your memory through all generations;
therefore the nations will praise you for ever and ever.

As you read the book, come and see that the King is more majestic than you imagined, your role as His Bride is more special than you dreamed, and your role in His Kingdom is more important than you know.

For me, knowing the Lord as my King and Bridegroom has brought incredible freedom and joy. It has been an intimate journey of awe and discovery. I have become even more passionate (those who know me say it isn't possible!) and I have learned to trust Him to take many steps of faith. (Be sure to read the epilogue to hear the story of my most recent adventure with the Lord.) My love for His people all over the world has grown deeper, and I have seen that it is only through our intimate partnership with the Lord that the nations will be reached with the gospel.

As you read, let the truth of God's love sink into your heart. The fairy tale is real, and it is just beginning.

"'Come!' say the Spirit and the Bride. Whoever hears, echo, 'Come!' Is anyone thirsty? 'Come!' All who will, come and drink. Drink freely of the water of life."

Revelation 22:17

My prayer for you...

As you embark on this journey with *The King and I*, I pray it will become very personal to you. May your heart quicken as you encounter your awesome heavenly Bridegroom in His majesty and power. Consider your love story with Him as either just beginning or being freshly ignited. My prayer is that your passion for Jesus would draw you to pursue Him and His purposes for our generation. Indeed, He is a passionate lover who delights in romancing His bride with ever-increasing revelations of His indescribable nature.

This dance of grace and glory will sweep us into a love for the lost and a desire to see Him made famous in the nations. He tenderly leads His Bride as you dance to His love song echoing throughout the earth calling forth the completion of His Bride.

May our awesome and intimate King Jesus be glorified as we dance with Him! "Take me away with you, let us hurry! Let the king bring me into his chambers" (Song of Songs 1:4).

With love and prayers,

Nancy

The King

How awesome is the Lord Most High,
the great King over all the earth!...
For God is the King of all the earth;
sing to him a psalm of praise.
God reigns over all the nations;
God is seated on his holy throne."

Psalm 47:2,7&8

Chapter 1

Captivated by the King

"My heart is stirred by a noble theme
as I recite my verses for the king;
my tongue is the pen of a skillful writer.
You are the most excellent of men and your lips
have been anointed with grace,
since God has blessed you forever."

Psalm 45:1-2

"The King is coming," they announced, "His Majesty, the King of Togo is coming to this hotel!"

I was in Miami, Florida, with a high school mission trip to the inner city, when we suddenly heard the news. A king was coming! Although many people had never heard of Togo, the tiny West African country, they scurried around getting ready for its king. Preparations were being made quickly, floors scoured and buffed to a shine. There was a flurry of activity to present the perfect environment for the king.

And it was worth it when he came. With his entourage of people and his African robes, he was enchanting. He was even a Christian, and shared his story with our group. He had the true heart of a leader – strong, compassionate and bold.

But my thoughts soon drifted to our own King, the King of the Universe. Are we enchanted with the Lord? We go to Him with requests when we want something. We offer a passing "thanks" when things go well, but are we captivated by Him? Have we lost our sense of wonder and reverent awe for our awesome and intimate King?

In Hawaii, the only state in the U.S. that still holds annual ceremonies to honor past kings, I visited the former royal palace. I was amazed at the beauty and ceremony surrounding the kings and queens of Hawaii. In terms of ceremony and pageantry, no reign surpassed King Kalakaua's, who was crowned King of Hawaii in 1883.

Picture this: he and his queen had two richly jeweled crowns of solid gold (15 and 18 carats fine). Each crown was studded with real gems like diamonds, opals, emeralds, rubies and pearls. The king wore a gold coronation ring of red onyx and diamonds, and held a scepter of fine silver, richly gilt with pure gold.

During the coronation ceremony, the royal family was led by 7-year-old Princess Kaiulani, a niece of the king, followed by other royal ladies in stunning royal attire. Princess Liliuokalani, the king's sister and heiress, wore a gown made of Parisian gold and white brocaded silk. Her headdress had delicate white feathers tipped with pearls and gold leaves, and she wore diamond earrings and a gold necklace with a diamond cross. After all, she was the future queen.

Last to appear were the stars of the day, their Majesties King Kalakaua and Queen Kapiolani. After the ceremony opened with a hymn, the grand marshal presented the king to his people, using his full name and various titles (20 or more), based on his deeds and accomplishments.

After the presentation, the king received his sword as the "Ensign of Justice and Mercy," his royal mantle as an "Ensign of Knowledge and Wisdom," his ring as an "Ensign of Kingly Dignity," and the scepter, as an "Ensign of Kingly Power and Justice." The scepter, nearly two and a half feet long, was surmounted by a globe and a dove of peace.

The climax of the ceremony was the crowning of the king. The crown was handed to him by a minister, saying, "Receive this crown of pure gold to adorn the high station wherein thou hast been placed." Placing it on his head himself, because no one else was worthy, he then placed a similar but smaller crown upon the queen's head "to share the honors of my throne."

In our current culture, we have lost the awe of royalty. We hear about ancient rulers, or see glimpses of royalty in foreign countries, but we wouldn't know what to do if we were suddenly given a king. We wouldn't want a sovereign power over our lives. We would still want to do things our way.

When I was a college freshman, I had built my own kingdom. I sought relationships that I thought would give me love. I sought rewards that I thought would give me significance. I even sought religion, because I thought it would give me righteousness. In my kingdom, I was the center of my world, and my image was built on earthly satisfaction and success.

But deep down, I knew I was only in captivity to my own desires. My heart longed for more.

On the outside, I presented a perfect image. Inside, my world was crumbling. My life spiraled out of control through a secretive eating disorder. One Sunday, I was in church with a hangover, and I cried out to God in desperation, "Please show me how to know You. I need help!"

Later when I heard the simple powerful Gospel message, it was like receiving an amazing and indescribable gift that I did not deserve. I was literally transferred from the kingdom of darkness to the kingdom of God, and I have come to realize that the heart of our Savior is to "seek and save the lost." If you have not heard the message or received Jesus as your Savior, I invite you to turn to page 146 at the back now, and read about "The Eternal Love Story."

When we understand that the Lord is not a fallible earthly king, it becomes much easier to trust Him with our lives. Compare King Kalakaua's coronation with the image of Christ's throne that John records in the book of Revelation.

"At once I was in the Spirit, and there before me was a throne in heaven with someone sitting on it. And the one who sat there had the appearance of jasper and carnelian. A rainbow, resembling an emerald, encircled the throne. Surrounding the throne were twenty-four other thrones, and seated on them were twenty-four elders. They were dressed in white and had crowns of gold on their heads. From the throne came flashes of lightning, rumblings and peals of thunder. Before the throne, seven lamps were blazing. These are the seven spirits of God. Also before the throne there was what looked like a sea of glass, clear as crystal.

"In the center, around the throne, were four living creatures, and they were covered with eyes, in front and in back. The first living creature was like a lion, the second was like an ox, the third had a face like a man, the fourth was like a flying eagle. Each of the four living creatures had six wings and was covered with eyes all around, even under his wings. Day and night they never stop saying: 'Holy, holy, holy is the Lord God Almighty, who was, and is, and is to come'" (Revelation 4:2-8).

The more I spend time with the Lord, the more amazed I become at His love that never ends. I am no longer held captive by my own desires. Knowing Jesus, the most magnificent, glorious King, captivates me in the best way. I am continually in awe at the new discoveries I make about His indescribable beauty and greatness.

To be captivated by the King is to have eyes for Him alone. To desire His pleasure, His favor and His will more than anything the world has to offer. In that adoring gaze, a transformation occurs. Our life begins to be about our King instead of about ourselves. It's been an exciting journey for me since my days in college, and I pray that this will be the beginning or renewing of an amazing journey for you.

Personal Reflection

- How would it make you feel to have an earthly king? What about a perfect, heavenly one?
- How do you picture God's throne? Make a drawing of what it might look like. Personalize it.
- Write out a prayer to the Lord. Ask him to reveal Himself to you or to open your heart. Ask Him to captivate your heart in a fresh and intimate way.

Crown Jewel: Psalm 89:6

"For who in the skies above can compare with the Lord?

Who is like the Lord among the heavenly beings?"

King Over All The Earth

(based on Zech. 14:4,5,9)

Kings and kingdoms will all pass away!
His feet shall stand in that day;

The Lord my God shall come,
Long-awaited, desired One.

Upon the Mount of Olives He stands,
The saints follow as He commands;

King of Kings shall reign,
All the earth to gain;

Glory, majesty and praise,
A victory banner we'll raise;

Every knee will bow,
and tongue confess:

Jesus, One Lord and King,
Let every heart and soul sing!

Even so, come Lord Jesus!

~ NW ~

Chapter 2

Clothed with Majesty

"Gird your sword upon your side, O Mighty One;
clothe Yourself with splendor and majesty.
In Your majesty ride forth victoriously in behalf of
truth, humility and righteousness;
let Your right hand display awesome deeds."

Psalm 45:3-4

When we heard the King of Togo was coming to our hotel in Miami, immediate excitement filled the rooms. The high school students on the mission trip were thrilled, and they began getting ready. They were going to meet the king!

That morning, I went out for an early morning swim in the ocean. Basking in the beauty and serenity of the calm sea, I was lost to everything around me. I was swimming far out to see if I could spot some dolphins, when suddenly a blow horn interrupted my tranquility.

"Get in now! All swimmers in now!"

My first thought was sharks, so I swam as fast as I could to shore. The beach patrol was there to greet me. "Lady, you've been contaminated!" they said, "There's been a sewage spill. You better get cleaned up fast."

Contaminated?! I was shocked, and hurried off to shower, but the hotel was guarded in preparation for the king. When I went to the door of the hotel lobby, a security officer wouldn't let me pass.

"Lady, don't you know the king is coming?" he said gruffly, "You can't come in here. You'll have to go in through the parking garage." I felt unworthy to even be staying in the same hotel as the king.

He was royalty, and I was contaminated.

I eventually got cleaned up, but the experience had given me a visual example of how glorious our great King is compared to our unworthiness.

"Who may ascend the hill of the Lord?" says Psalm 24, "Who may stand in his holy place? He who has clean hands and a pure heart, who does not lift up his soul to an idol or swear by what is false. He will receive blessing from the Lord and vindication from God his Savior" (Psalm 24:3-5).

The more we see God's majestic holiness, the more we see our true condition.

The prophet Isaiah was given a glimpse of God's glory like John was in Revelation. Isaiah writes,

"...I saw the Lord seated on a throne, high and exalted, and the train of his robe filled the temple. Above him were seraphs, each with six wings: With two wings they covered their faces, with two they covered their feet, and with two they were flying. And they were calling to one another:

'Holy, holy, holy is the LORD Almighty;
the whole earth is full of his glory.'

At the sound of their voices the doorposts and thresholds
shook and the temple was filled with smoke"
(Isaiah 6:1-4).

At seeing this sight, Isaiah was overcome by his own sin. "I am a man of unclean lips," he cried, "and I live among a people of unclean lips" (v. 5).

The Lord's clothing is not an earthly fabric, but it is His holiness and glory. We cannot compare.

When Adam and Eve first sinned, they hid themselves from the Lord, and made clothing to cover themselves. Compared to God's holiness, they felt unworthy and shameful. He could have left us all like that. Alone, disgraced, forsaken. But God had a bigger plan, and He sent Christ to redeem His Church. He brought new clothing and prepared a place of honor for us. And He invites us into a relationship with Him.

But so many people miss the opportunity. They shun God,

wanting to control their own lives. They don't want a king. They have missed seeing His greatness and majesty. They fear that God is like the kings of the past, seeking only their own glory.

When I was in Istanbul, Turkey, I went to pray in Topkapi Palace, the place where the Sultans formerly reigned. I wanted to understand the past royal kingdom, and I learned about the ultimate power exerted by the Sultan. He required all his ambassadors to bow down and kiss the hem of his robe, and he exerted sovereign rule from his throne. He demanded honor, respect and loyalty. Then he died, and the next Sultan demanded the same things.

But the Lord is different. His greatness and majesty are perfect, and they last forever. God doesn't need to seek His own glory. It is a part of who He is. As the prophet Habakkuk writes, "His glory covered the heavens and His praise filled the earth. His splendor was like the sunrise; rays flashed from His hand, where His power was hidden...He stood, and shook the earth; he looked, and made the nations tremble. The ancient mountains crumbled and the age-old hills collapsed. His ways are eternal" (Habakkuk 3:3,4,6).

As I have traveled all over the world, I have seen His awesome deeds. He is a noble, just, worthy, righteous and victorious King. He loves His people and defends those who call upon Him in humility and truth.

As the chorus of the old song goes, "kings and kingdoms will all pass away, but there's something about that Name!"

We should desire to come before the King and worship His majesty, especially because of what happens when we do. He welcomes us. He forgives us. Our resplendent King Jesus has clothed us with His very own garment of salvation and arrayed us with His robe of righteousness.

When Christ was having dinner at one of the Pharisees homes, a woman "who lived a sinful life," possibly a prostitute, came into the room and brought an alabaster vial of perfume. "... And as she stood behind him at his feet weeping, she began to wet his feet with her tears. Then she wiped them with her hair, kissed them and poured perfume on them" (Luke 7:38).

This woman understood Christ's holiness and honor. Love flowed from her, with no thought of the approval of man. Her eyes were set on one person, Jesus. Her passion was fueled by His irresistible grace and forgiveness. She knew she was completely unworthy to be there, but she wanted to worship Him. He deserved it.

But the Pharisees were shocked and they criticized Jesus. He responded to them by saying, "...You did not give me any water for my feet, but she wet my feet with her tears and wiped them with her hair. You did not give me a kiss, but this woman, from the time I entered, has not stopped kissing my feet. You did not put oil on my head, but she has poured perfume on my feet. Therefore, I tell you, her many sins have been forgiven—for she loved much. But he who has been forgiven little loves little.' Then Jesus said to her, 'Your sins are forgiven'" (Luke 7:44-48).

When we come before God, knowing our sin and unworthiness, it pleases Him to accept us and elevate us to a higher status than we deserve. He longs for us to trust Him as King.

Personal Reflection

- What has stopped you from viewing God as King?
- Is it hard for you to trust Him as King of your life? What areas are you still trying to control?
- Take some time to pray.

  PRAISE God for His majesty.

  WORSHIP Him for His holiness and for His presence with you.

  ASK Him to cleanse you of anything you have put before Him.

  CONFESS any sin to Him to forgive and set you free!

  RECEIVE His affection and intimate love for you!

Crown Jewel: Isaiah 66:1-2

"This is what the Lord says, 'Heaven is my throne,
and the earth is my footstool.
Where is the house you will build for me?
Where will my resting place be?
Has not my hand made all these things,
and so they came into being?' declares the Lord."

My Regal King

One so high and glorious is He,
Yet in human likeness came to be;
Born of a virgin birth,
Such incredible worth;
Prophesied long ago,
He wanted us to know—
He is our King of glory,
Author of every story;
Humbly riding on a donkey,
What a wonder to me;
My regal King of Kings
To whom all creation sings;
Chose to dwell within my heart,
And give me a brand new start;
His beauty and majesty captivates,
From His throne it radiates;
The cradle and the cross,
Overcame our loss;
Mary chose to believe
And humbly receive

Angels declared "Glory to God in the Highest
And on earth peace to men on whom His favor rests"
John was a prophet of the Most High
He prepared the way with His cry;
What now is my role,
En route to my heavenly goal?
Jesus, Jesus I proclaim,
The power of Your matchless name!
I lift You up for all to see,
My Bridegroom—King eternally!

NW
~ December 6, 2002 ~

Chapter 3

Conquering King

*"Let Your sharp arrows pierce the hearts
of the king's enemies;
let the nations fall beneath Your feet."*

Psalm 45:5

For centuries, kings have ridden into battle with their armies. Some have been good kings, some bad. King Arthur, Genghis Khan, Alexander the Great, Henry V. In many countries, a king's success was measured by his ability to conquer.

When Christ came, He never raised a sword, but He is still known as a conquering king. He defeated death. He defeated sin. He crushed the forces that no human being had ever been able to win against.

In my life, God has proven Himself stronger than my addictive eating disorder, breaking through the spiritual chains that held me captive. He has also given me a spirit of power. Christ has given us His Holy Spirit to fill and empower us to be His witnesses and to conquer evil in His name. "But you will receive power when the Holy Spirit comes on you; and you will be my witnesses in Jerusalem, and in all Judea and Samaria, and to the ends of the earth" (Acts 1:8). All over the world, our King is showing His glory. Through the prayers and faith of His people, our King is bursting through.

Think about some of the names Christ is known by. Many are related to His ability to triumph – over sin, over the forces of the world, over our own inadequacies. Take a minute to thank God for some of his victorious titles.

Almighty One
"'I am the Alpha and the Omega,' says the Lord God, 'who is, and who was, and who is to come, the Almighty'" (Revelation 1:8).

Arm of the Lord
"Awake, awake! Clothe yourself with strength, O arm of the LORD; awake, as in days gone by, as in generations of old…" (Isaiah 51:9).

Deliverer
"And so all Israel will be saved, as it is written: "The deliverer will come from Zion; he will turn godlessness away from Jacob" (Romans 11:26).

Eternal King
"Now to the King eternal, immortal, invisible, the only God, be honor and glory for ever and ever. Amen" (1 Timothy 1:17).

Guardian of our Souls
"For you were like sheep going astray, but now you have returned to the Shepherd and Overseer of your souls" (I Peter 2:25).

Head of the Church
"And God placed all things under his feet and appointed him to be head over everything for the church" (Ephesians 1:22).

Horn of Salvation
"He has raised up a horn of salvation for us in the house of his servant David" (Luke 1:69).

King
"Rejoice greatly, O Daughter of Zion! Shout, Daughter of Jerusalem! See, your king comes to you, righteous and having salvation, gentle and riding on a donkey, on a colt, the foal of a donkey" (Zechariah 9:9).

King of kings
"…God, the blessed and only Ruler, the King of kings and Lord of lords" (I Timothy 6:15).

King of the Ages
…"Great and marvelous are your deeds, Lord God Almighty. Just and true are your ways, King of the ages" (Revelation 15:3).

Leader
"See, I have made him a witness to the peoples, a leader and commander of the peoples" (Isaiah 55:4).

Lion of the Tribe of Judah
"Then one of the elders said to me, 'Do not weep! See, the Lion of the tribe of Judah, the Root of David, has triumphed. He is able to open the scroll and its seven seals'" (Revelation 5:5).

Lord of lords
"…God, the blessed and only Ruler, the King of kings and Lord of lords" (I Timothy 6:15).

Lord Our Righteousness
"In his days Judah will be saved and Israel will live in safety. This is the name by which he will be called: The LORD Our Righteousness" (Jeremiah 23:6).

Mighty God
"For to us a child is born, to us a son is given, and the government will be on his shoulders. And he will be called Wonderful Counselor, Mighty God, Everlasting Father, Prince of Peace" (Isaiah 9:6).

Rock
"They all ate the same spiritual food and drank the same spiritual drink; for they drank from the spiritual rock that accompanied them, and that rock was Christ" (I Corinthians 10:3-4).

Ruler of God's Creation
"To the angel of the church in Laodicea write: These are the words of the Amen, the faithful and true witness, the ruler of God's creation" (Revelation 3:14).

Ruler of Kings
"And from Jesus Christ, who is the faithful witness, the firstborn from the dead, and the ruler of the kings of the earth" (Revelation 1:5).

A few years ago, as I was preparing to lead a mission team of high school and college students to Bulgaria, we encountered several barriers. It seemed like it would be very difficult to do the things other groups had done in the past, like having students go into high school classrooms to talk about values, including personal faith in Christ. There was also hesitation to try new things, caused by fear and unbelief.

So we sought the Lord as a team, and prayed often for the trip. I was praying against these causes when God showed me a new name for Himself – God of the Breakthrough.

In 2 Samuel 5:17-20, the Philistines were pursing David, so he went down to the stronghold and inquired of the Lord. "… 'Shall I go and attack the Philistines? Will you hand them over to me?' The Lord answered him, 'Go, for I will surely hand the Philistines over to you.' So David went to Baal Perazim and there he defeated them. He said, 'As waters break out, the Lord has broken out against my enemies before me'…" (2 Samuel 5:19-20).

Baal Perazim means "The Master of the breakthrough" or "The God who bursts through."

In Bulgaria, the Lord gave us fresh boldness and zeal in evangelism. Our confidence was in the power of the gospel and the "Master of the breakthrough." Our team worshipped Him each day, and we prayed bold prayers for Him to open doors, hearts and minds for the gospel. "…The reason the Son of God appeared was to destroy the devil's work" (1 John 3:8).

And God did. We were able to go into classrooms that we thought would not let us in. The Lord gave fresh vision to the believers in Bulgaria, and He showed us the power of the gospel and believing prayer. About 40-50 students prayed and received Christ. Almost all of our translators received Christ with us, three of them on Good Friday. Creativity blossomed. The students created a band, and I got to give a gospel message after they had performed at a nightclub.

God also did some amazing breakthroughs in families; one entire family came to Jesus. My translator, a girl named Donny, told me her mother was dying of a brain tumor and her father was very angry with God.

So I went to pray for them, along with Ken, my co-leader, and God touched their hearts with His love and truth. Her father and her sister received Jesus while we were visiting their house. Then her mother, Valia, who had been moaning, sudden-ly said she wanted to sit up. After explaining the gospel to her, Donny and I also prayed with her as she received Christ.

Donny's father began to grow in his faith, and Donny told me he had become a new man. He no longer felt distressed and worried, and he knew his wife was in Jesus' care. On the day I left Bulgaria, Valia died and went to be with her Lord.

Our King, Christ desires to rule supreme in our lives, so that we can experience His victory. He wants us to crown Him King and sovereign Lord over our lives. He wants to break through!

Personal Reflection

- What do you need God to conquer in your life?
- Where do you need God to breakthrough? A personal struggle, a people group you are praying for, our nation? Pray specifically for areas and nations that need our Conquering King to burst through.
- Who could you pray for that needs a breakthrough in their own life?

Crown Jewel: 1 John 5:4-5

"…This is the victory that has overcome the world,
even our faith.
Who is it that overcomes the world? Only he who believes that
Jesus is the Son of God."

Easter Sunday

The stone is rolled away, New life breaks forth today;
The Victory You've won, A mighty work is done;
All creation celebrates, The whole world reverberates;
Mountains and hills sing, With a jubilant ring;
The sun beams down, With Your glory and renown;
All the trees clap their hands, Rejoicing at Your commands;
The rain and snow water the earth, Reminding me of new birth;
Seeds have been sown, Making Your name known;
You make them flourish, Your children will nourish;
Accomplishing what You desire, Igniting a holy fire;
Your bread was broken, The Word has spoken;
Rivers of life are flowing, As we continue sowing!
Lead us on in joy and peace, More captives to release!
Soon I'll see Your face, Enjoying forever Your embrace;
'Til that day I'll press on, By Your Spirit all are drawn;
A multitude to bring my King, So they can forever sing!
Hallelujah, Jesus reigns!
No unbended knee remains!

NW
April 11, 2004, Sophia, Bulgaria

Chapter 4

Compassionate Savior

"You love righteousness and hate wickedness;
therefore God, your God, has set you above your com-
panions by anointing you with the oil of joy.
All your robes are fragrant with myrrh and aloes and
cassia; from palaces adorned with ivory the music of
the strings makes you glad."

Psalm 45:7-8

King David was called "a man after God's own heart" (Samuel 13:14), yet at various times in his life, he was guilty of sin and disobedience toward God. But what set David apart from other kings was how he always came back to God. He always admitted his sin, confessing with a contrite heart (Psalm 51:17).

David seemed to have learned something about God from his early days as a shepherd. No matter how many times his sheep ran away, he always brought them back. He always cared for them. He always loved them. In the New Testament, Christ refers to Himself as the Good Shepherd, and gives several illustrations of His people being like sheep (John 10:1-19).

When we were leaving the village in Bulgaria with Donny, my translator, we met a young shepherd in the street. I was overjoyed, because I had always wanted to meet a real shepherd. So we stopped to talk with Thomas, but his sheep were afraid of us and ran the other way. Yet when they heard his voice, they came quickly to his side.

"Do they each have names?" I asked him. He immediately called, "Dahlia, come here," and the sheep came. "Sasha, come here," and another came. It was so intimate and touching. Jesus words came to my mind, "My sheep listen to my voice; I know them, and they follow me. I give them eternal life, and they shall never perish; no one can snatch them out of my hand" (John 10:27-28).

As I petted the sheep, securely next to Thomas, I asked him if he knew the Good Shepherd, Jesus. He did not, and I was able to talk to him about my personal Shepherd.

It was the perfect illustration of Christ's heart to rescue lost sheep, wherever they are. God's timing is so amazing and tender, "…not wanting any to perish, but everyone to come to repentance" (2 Peter 3:9). He is full of compassion and His love for His people overflows.

I saw Christ's love come alive when I watched Mel Gibson's movie "The Passion of the Christ." It gripped my heart and emotions with indelible force. I saw my beloved Jesus pouring every drop of His blood to purchase His Bride, the Church. Never has there been such sacrificial love. The great King of glory took on human flesh, only to suffer immeasurable wounds as He bore every imaginable sin and human atrocity.

Throughout the film, my heart was wrenched in agony and awe. I saw the incredible, powerful, courageous and regal love demonstrated before my very eyes. Every part of Jesus' body was covered with blood, as a visual picture of a sacrificial lamb being led to slaughter. Jesus fulfilled the Jewish sacrificial system when he offered Himself as the "…Lamb of God, who takes away the sins of the world" (John 1:29).

In those tear-stained heart piercing moments, all I could think of was my precious Savior's love for every person in the entire world.

The late Bill Bright put it this way, "It is unthinkable that an earthly sovereign like Queen Elizabeth II would put aside her jewels and dress in rags. But that is exactly what God did. When Jesus Christ was born in a drafty stable, the only people who worshipped him were lowly shepherds."

The word "passion" has several different meanings. It can mean a deep longing for something, or striving after a specific goal. It is also directly used to describe Christ's death on the cross. In Mel Gibson's film, the definitions are combined. Christ loved us with such intensity that He laid down His life to save us.

In Bulgaria, we took 50 teenagers to see "The Passion of the Christ." It was a touching experience for each person, especially two of our translators. They had been spending an inordinate amount of time with each other, with a lot of physical affection. We had been witnessing to them and praying for them, but when they saw Jesus' sacrificial love on the cross, it deeply touched their hearts.

Weeping, they confessed to a member of our team, "we are sinners!" In the light of Christ's beauty, they saw their sin. They saw that they could never stand before a holy God without having the Savior's blood to cover their sin. His costly sacrifice had purchased their freedom from sin and bondage. They understood the gospel, and eagerly received this gift of forgiveness of sin and new life in Jesus Christ.

They finally understood love. "This is love: not that we loved God, but that He loved us and sent His Son as an atoning sacrifice for our sins" (1 John 4:10).

It was an incredible evening of rejoicing with our translators, as well as other new believers. Never will I get over the joy of seeing one sinner repent. Like the angels in heaven, we can praise the victory of our compassionate Savior.

As I was writing this passage, contemplating Christ's love for the lost, I was suddenly interrupted. A man was climbing up a ladder to do maintenance work near the porch where I was sitting. I had to smile at our Savior's love. Just when I thought I was all alone, He brought someone right to me so that we could talk about the King. There are no lengths God will not go to for just one person to come to know him.

Personal Reflection

- What are you passionate about?
- Does Christ's passion elicit passion in your own heart? Pray that He would strengthen that passion.
- List some people to pray for, that they would know our Savior's great love.

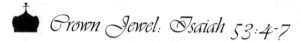 *Crown Jewel: Isaiah 53:4-7*

Surely he took up our infirmities
and carried our sorrows,
yet we considered him stricken by God,
smitten by him, and afflicted.
But he was pierced for our transgressions,
he was crushed for our iniquities;
the punishment that brought us peace was upon him,
and by his wounds we are healed.

My Suffering Savior

The depth of my sin is ever before me;
Faced with Your suffering again I see;
The wickedness of all my pride,
In my self-righteousness I try to hide;
But oh, Your precious blood was shed, To cover my sin,
Declaring my old self dead;
What victory I can declare, For in Your life, I now share;
You have conquered over sin,
And all my bandages that have been;
My Spirit and soul are set free, A new creation, that is me!
Now I live in joyful union, Relishing intimate communion;
Receive my fresh dedication, To live for Your affirmation;
My joy, my love, my source of all, On You I will continually call;
Save me from anything less,
Than growing in grace and godliness;
To proclaim the glory of Your name,
And spread Your irresistible fame;
For people and nations must hear,
About Yeshua, My Savior, so dear!
"Unquenchable fire" I pray, Holy Spirit, have Your way!
Abba, Father, reveal your power, In this final decisive hour!
Behold, I am coming soon!
Jesus, Your words I attune!

NW
~ February 25, 2004, Ash Wednesday ~

∵ *45* ∵

His Bride

"'In that day,' declares the Lord, 'you will call me "my husband"; you will no longer call me "my master"...
I will betroth you in righteousness and justice,
in love and compassion. I will betroth you in
faithfulness, and you will acknowledge the Lord."
Hosea 2:16,19 & 20

Chapter 5

Crowned with Honor

"Daughters of kings are among your honored women;
at your right hand is the royal bride in gold of Ophir.
Listen, O daughter, consider and give ear:
Forget your people and your father's house."

Psalm 45:9-10

The crown.

The final adornment. The symbol to convey the position, to top off the ceremony and show the world this was someone very important. It should be big and bright and covered with jewels. Surely that was the sign of true royalty.

But our King's earthly crown was a crown of thorns. It was painful. It was ugly. And Christ wore it so that one day we could wear the crown of righteousness.

He calls the Church His Bride.

He rescued us from an eternity of endless agony apart from Him and then elevated us to the status of being His royal Bride. He declares, "You will be a crown of splendor in the Lord's hand, a royal diadem in the hand of your God" (Isaiah 62:3-5).

Imagine a crown on your head. We don't see many crowns nowadays that aren't from Burger King or part of a Halloween costume, but just imagine that you are part of a royal court where a crown is expected and required. What would it look like? Gold and sparkling? Would it have rubies? Emeralds? Diamonds?

How would the crown make you feel? Would you sit up a little taller? Feel a little more respected, valued, special?

Christ has given us a crown. He has claimed us as His Bride.

Together with other believers, we have been chosen. Think about the lyrics from the old hymn, "The Church's One Foundation."

The Church's one Foundation is Jesus Christ Her Lord,
She is His new creation by water and the Word.
From heaven He came and sought Her to be His holy Bride,
With His own blood He bought Her and for her life he died.

In Jewish bridal tradition, a bride price is paid to the father of the bride as the wedding arrangements are made. It is usually a large sum of money, denoting the value of the bride. For His Church, Christ paid the bride price with the most valuable of all gifts, His life. "For you know that it was not with perishable things such as silver or gold that you were redeemed from the empty way of life handed down to you from your forefathers, but with the precious blood of Christ, a lamb without blemish or defect" (1 Peter 1:18-19).

But so many people ignore this sacrifice, and they turn away from Christ. They may never have truly understood or heard of His sacrificial love for them. Some won't accept His gift, or they continue to live like they have not been redeemed, like they have not been set free from everything that held them captive.

Consider Psalm 45, where the bride is reminded to "Listen, O daughter, consider and give ear: Forget your people and your father's house" (Psalm 45:10). She is about to start a new life, a royal life. She needs to forget her past and assume her new role. If she continued to look back, she would lose the joy set before her.

We need to do the same. For many women, the past is full of hurt, bitterness, pain and shame. Jesus knows and cares, and came to deliver and heal us. We are now of royal lineage, and there is about to be a transformation.

The key is to know who you are. You are the daughter of the King of kings. You are a loved, honored woman, soon to be the co-regent of the universe as the Bride of Christ, to rule and reign for all eternity. Do you treat yourself like this is true? "Do you not know that your body is a temple of the Holy Spirit, who is in you, whom you have received from God? You are not your own: you were bought with a price. Therefore honor God with your body" (1 Corinthians 6:19-20). Your earthly body is now a tabernacle for the King, who sits on the throne of your life. You are a picture frame for the world to see Jesus.

I met a woman in Hawaii who had a hard time letting go of things and giving them to God. I passed by her house every day on my way to the beach (before I knew her) and I always noticed the sign.

"Custom bikinis for sale, made in 24 hours."

Then one day I was walking on the beach, and a lady and her dog came by. Just as quickly as I greeted her, she tripped over the remains of a sand castle. Eager to help, I asked if she was okay, and we started talking. Her name was Anita, and she was the bikini designer.

Every time after that, when I walked by her home, I would pray for her. She said she lived with a guy named Joe, so I prayed for him, too. Then one evening, she saw me and we walked together. She opened up about her life and some of her hurts. Her sand castle really had crumbled. Joe was out of town and she was lonely, so she invited me for coffee the next morning. As we visited, my prayers began to be answered. She opened up about her abuse by her past husband, deception from "so-called" Christians, and being ripped off by those she tried to help.

She had so much hurt, and she hadn't let go of it yet. My heart still aches for Anita. I continue to pray that Jesus' love will heal her heart. We have built a special friendship, and I know in God's time He will show her too, that she can trust His love.

But compare Anita with the character of Danielle in the movie "Ever After," a rendition of Cinderella. Locked in the prison of her cruel stepmother's control, Danielle is made to dress in rags, while her evil stepsisters are treated to the finery that once belonged to her.

Lost in her shame and degradation, she had been robbed of her true identity. Yet the prince found her in her brokenness and set his affection and desire upon her, pursuing her with relentless determination.

At the end of the movie, an evil suitor has taken Danielle captive, but the prince finds her. Though she is dressed in rags and he in royal robes, he tenderly kneels to propose to her. In a life-changing moment, she chooses to say, "yes" to be his bride and queen.

The next time the audience sees Danielle, she is wearing a glorious crown.

Someday soon, we will have the great jewels of a crown. Our crowning headpiece signifies our consecration to be "set apart" for our Bridegroom and our future glory. "Now there is in store for me the crown of righteousness, which the Lord, the righteous Judge, will award to me on that day—and not only to me, but also to all who have longed for His appearing" (2 Timothy 4:8).

Imagine a bride preparing for her wedding day. A dear friend of mine, soon to be married, described her wedding gown to me. She said, "It's so gorgeous! I thought I was going to choose something simple, but when I put on this extravagantly embroidered dress, it took my breath away! I knew it was just for me!"

In a similar way, our wedding gown is being prepared for us with intricate detail. As we anticipate our wedding day, our character is being developed and purified through the fires of life. The end product will be a magnificent gold as we glisten with the attributes of God.

Embroidery work is being added daily through enhancing, magnifying and adding color in every experience of our lives. We might not always see it, or we might see the confusing underside of the fabric, but the beauty will be revealed in God's perfect timing. Until that glorious day, let us prepare for our King. One day we will lay our crown at His feet in awe and adoration.

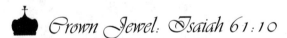

Personal Reflection

- What is the pain in your life which you have trouble letting go? Take some time to pray and give it over to God.
- What changes about you when you think of yourself with a crown? What stops you from thinking that way all the time?
- Meditate on Zephaniah 3:14-17 and Isaiah 61:10 and praise Jesus for delighting in you.

"Sing, O Daughter of Zion; shout aloud, O Israel! Be glad and rejoice with all your heart, O Daughter of Jerusalem! The Lord has taken away your punishment, he has turned back your enemy. The Lord, the King of Israel, is with you; never again will you fear any harm. On that day they will say to Jerusalem, 'Do not fear, O Zion; do not let your hands hang limp. The Lord your God is with you, He is mighty to save. He will take great delight in you, he will quiet you with His love, He will rejoice over you with singing'" (Zephaniah 3:14-17).

Crown Jewel: Isaiah 61:10

"I delight greatly in the Lord; my soul rejoices in my God.
For He has clothed me with garments of salvation
and arrayed me in a robe of righteousness,
as a bridegroom adorns his head like a priest,
and as a bride adorns herself with her jewels."

My Bridegroom

Bridegroom of my soul,
You have made me whole;
Lover of my very being,
Knowing You is seeing;
You've opened my eyes,
Heard all my cries;
Delivered me from despair,
In Your intimate care;
As You paid my Bride price,
I became born twice;
Costly crown of glory,
Began my new story;
Because You were slain,
With You one day I'll reign;
My crown at Your feet,
As I take my royal seat;
My true identity has begun,
United with You I run;
Delighting in Your grace,
Gazing in Your face;
I'm passionately enraptured,
My heart You have captured.
Crowned by my King,
My life to You I bring.

NW
~ May 24, 2003 ~

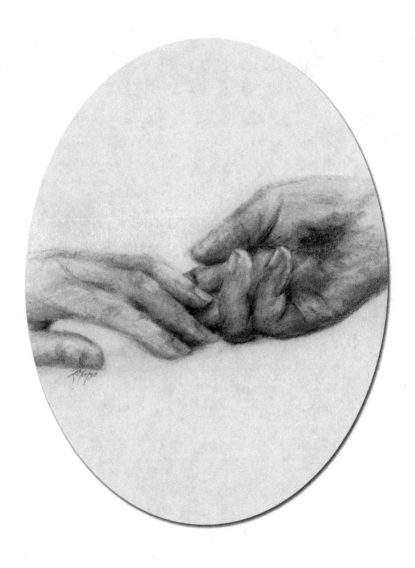

Chapter 6

Chosen for Intimacy

"The king is enthralled by your beauty;
honor him, for he is your lord.
The Daughter of Tyre will come with a gift,
men of wealth will seek your favor."

Psalm 45:11-12

I met Simge at an airport in Istanbul, Turkey. Delightful and vivacious, she had a friendly charm about her. Decked in the latest expensive fashion, she was my first acquaintance with the "modern" Turkish woman.

Countless conversations with young women in this Muslim country helped me understand their struggles and share their dreams. I longed and prayed for them to know the Lover of their souls.

One evening after a class in conversational English, Simge and I had tea. I gave her a book I wrote called, "In Pursuit of the Ideal," which deals with a woman's image, identity and intimacy. She proudly announced, "I will bring my picture for you! I used to look like Princess Monaco, but not anymore, I'm too fat!"

I immediately tried to reassure her, but she could not be dissuaded. In her mind, she was no longer beautiful as before, and she assumed that was why she was not married.

Simge was expressing one of the deepest longings of a woman's heart – to know she is beautiful. Every woman longs to know that she is cherished, valued and chosen by someone to love her exclusively. The bride described in Psalm 45 is given that reassurance. "The king is enthralled by your beauty" (Psalm 45:11).

To enthrall means, "to spellbind, fascinate." In Song of Songs, we see another picture of such pleasure in the bride. Her lover declares, "You have stolen my heart, my sister, my bride; you have stolen my heart with one glance of your eyes, with one jewel of your necklace" (Song of Songs 4:9).

The bride longed for intimacy with her beloved. Not just sexual intimacy, but complete social, emotional, mental and spiritual intimacy. Only in his presence did she fully experience the wonder of her truest identity, that of being his beautiful and beloved bride. I have discovered that Christ alone can convince our hearts of His intimate love for us. No amount of striving to earn His favor will do it. We must simply receive and rest in this heart revelation.

"What matters supremely," writes J.I. Packer, "is not...the fact that I know God, but the larger fact which underlies it – the fact that He knows me. I am engraved in the palm of His hands. I am never out of His mind."

The bridegroom in Song of Songs also praises his bride for having eyes like doves. "How beautiful you are, my darling! Oh, how beautiful! Your eyes are doves" (Song of Songs 1:15).

Not only is he admiring her beauty, but there is also symbolism in the verse. Doves have no peripheral vision; they can only see straight ahead and focus on one thing at a time. As we await our Bridegroom's return, He desires us to be faithful, to keep Him as our first love, cherishing Him exclusively. All other loves pale in comparison with Jesus.

When I was in college, I struggled to be free from the lifestyle I had before I accepted Jesus. I asked the woman who had led me to Christ for help. "How can I give up drinking, partying and guys?" I asked. She gently responded, "Focus on falling in love with Jesus."

Wow, I can do that, I thought. Jesus rescued me and gave everything for me - His very life. His love is irresistible and unconditional. Surely I can focus on that!

And my focus did change, opening the door for a beautiful dance with my Bridegroom. Little by little, I learned new steps, at times tripping over Him when I was trying to take over instead of trusting Him to lead. But the more I learned to trust, the more I fell in love with Him. What began as a simple dance has now become a beautiful, intimate partnership.

With each new dance, I've experienced His grace, picking me up when I fall down, or looking into my eyes when I feel like such a failure and reassuring me again of His delight in me with His embrace. He is truly incomparable.

Life and relationships can sometimes wound our sense of worth and value, particularly when we are face to face with our own inadequacy and sin. When faced with our sin and weakness, love always shows grace. My highest priority is to hear God's voice of affirmation and love, guidance and direction, to change me from within.

One stressful week, I was struggling with a particular relationship and felt anxious with all my responsibilities, so I planned a getaway with Jesus at my favorite place. I usually felt excited about my time with Him, but when I got there I was apprehensive.

Opening my Bible, I realized that instead of His tender love, I expected chastisement for my struggle. Internally, I cringed waiting for conviction and correction.

Then I heard a still, small voice encourage me to read the Song of Songs. As I began to read, the tears flowed. Never once in the Song of Songs did the lover criticize his bride. In spite of her flaws, he had only words of tender affection and praise for her. Oh what love, that embraces me apart from my imperfections and sees only my potential.

I think of the love expressed in *The Velveteen Rabbit*, who was loved so much, his dream came true to become real. But in the process, he lost his shiny outer fur and began to change.

"Weeks passed, and the little Rabbit grew very old and shabby, but the Boy loved him just as much. He loved him so hard that he loved all his whiskers off, and the pink lining to his ears turned grey, and his brown spots faded. He even began to lose his shape, and he scarcely looked like a rabbit any more, except to the Boy. To him he was always beautiful, and that was all that the little Rabbit cared about." (*The Velveteen Rabbit*, by Margery Williams)

The Rabbit began to change when he was loved and cared for by the Boy. The same happens with us. Just like the Rabbit lost his whiskers and shape, intimacy with Christ can sometimes feel painful. Masks are taken away, and pain and disappoint is revealed. But in our Bridegroom's total acceptance, the reward is much greater.

The Apostle Paul described everything else as loss compared to the surpassing greatness of knowing Christ Jesus (Philippians 3:8). Paul, a hero of mine, went on to say, "…forgetting what is behind and straining toward what is ahead, I press on toward the goal to win the prize for which God has called me heavenward in Christ Jesus" (Philippians 3:13,14).

I especially relate to Paul because I am single like he was, and have a unique call to serve Jesus solo. On most days, I cherish this privilege, to be concerned only with my Lord's affairs and be solely devoted to Him in body and spirit (1 Corinthians 7:34). I usually embrace my gift of singleness fully with joy.

But there are days when being a single woman is a challenge. Not only do I feel my aloneness, but at times am faced with my humanness, a desire for someone with skin and bones to cherish me. In the past, I often tried to stuff down my scary emotions, somehow thinking they would go away. But they always come out in one way or another if I don't deal with them.

The good news is that the Lord has used my brokenness to get my attention, resulting in my surrender and salvation. By God's grace, I am learning to take every thought captive to the obedience of Jesus (2 Corinthians 10:5). This frees me to face my fears and pain, as well as joy and delight. I'm learning the truth found in Psalm 73:25-26: "Whom have I in heaven but you? And earth has nothing I desire besides you. My flesh and my heart may fail, but God is the strength of my heart and my portion forever."

Life serves us a variety of menus, sometimes things we would not personally choose. Feelings of insecurity, unworthiness, or feeling far from beautiful, can sometimes overwhelm us. Our emotions can fluctuate daily, even hourly. But if we continually bring them to Jesus, He promises to draw us into His intimate love in a fresh way.

Personal Reflection

- How have you seen yourself start to change as you've trusted the Lord? What are areas of your life that you're hoping will change more?
- Think of your closest friendship. What makes you close? How is it different from your relationship with the Lord?
- Meditate on Psalm 139:13-18. How does it make you feel?

"For you created my inmost being; you knit me together in my mother's womb. I praise you because I am fearfully and wonderfully made; your works are wonderful, I know that full well. My frame was not hidden from you when I was made in the secret place. When I was woven together in the depths of the earth, your eyes saw my unformed body. All the days ordained for me were written in your book before one of them came to be. How precious to me are your thoughts, O God! How vast is the sum of them! Were I to count them, they would outnumber the grains of sand."

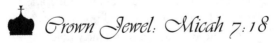

Crown Jewel: Micah 7:18

"Who is a God like you, who pardons sin and forgives the transgression of the remnant of his inheritance?
You do not stay angry forever but delight to show mercy."

Overwhelmed with Love

In my spirit I heard, "Come away,
You need my strengthening today;"
Feeling so aware of my weakness,
I came with some reluctance;
Would I be convicted of my sin,
Which always discouraged me within?
"Draw near to Me," You said,
"How beautiful you are," I read;
"Arise my darling, my beautiful one,"
And come with Me, the victory's won!
"All beautiful You are,
Majestic as a star!"
This Song of Songs is so sweet,
As I sit at my Savior's feet;
Overwhelming love so real,
Begins to change the way I feel!
Now I'm consumed by my Prince,
Who with His Words did convince;
"How delightful is your love, My sister, My bride,"
Learning to more fully abide at Your side;
His fiery love pierced my soul,
And once again made me whole.

NW
~ March 31, 2004, God's Place, Orlando, FL ~

Chapter 7

Chamber Intimacy

"All glorious is the princess within her chamber;
her gown is interwoven with gold.
In embroidered garments she is led to the king;
her virgin companions follow her and are brought to
you."

Psalm 45:13-14

In Istanbul, Turkey, I visited the Sultan's palace and got a glimpse of what it would be like to live in a harem. Outside the secluded quarters, young veiled women in dark brown burkas walked by, with only their faces showing. I thought about the story of Esther, who, centuries ago, was taken to the palace in Susa, Persia, to participate in a beauty contest. The winner would become queen.

A royal decree had gone out, ordering a search for beautiful young virgins for the king. In every province, commissioners were appointed to bring these girls into the harem at the citadel of Susa.

They were then placed under the care of Hegai, the king's eunuch, to oversee beauty treatments for twelve months in preparation to go into the king's presence.

Hadassah, known as Esther, was an orphan raised by her uncle Mordecai as his own daughter. She was lovely in form and features, and was taken to the king's palace and entrusted to Hegai. Her unusual beauty and demeanor pleased him and won his favor. Immediately, he gave her royal treatment, assigning her seven maids, special food and moved her to the best place in the harem.

Mordecai directed Esther not to tell anyone that she was a Jew.

Before a girl's turn came to go in to King Xerxes, she had to complete twelve months of beauty treatments, six months with the oil of myrrh and six with perfumes and cosmetics.

After her preparation period, she then would choose anything she wanted to take with her from the harem to the king's palace. In the evening, she would go to the king and in the morning return to another part of the harem, unless the king was pleased with her and called her by name (Esther 2:2-14 summarized).

Can you imagine the emotions that Esther felt? I'm sure a mixture of fear, anticipation, and awe to be going before the king, at that time the most powerful man in the world. What would her destiny hold? She had been selected for the most favored treatment, but would she become the next Queen of Persia? These thoughts were too mind-boggling, she had to simply wait, prepare and trust her sovereign king's decision.

Ultimately, she knew her destiny did not lie in the power of any earthly king, but only the Sovereign King of the Universe, her Jehovah. Esther, knowing her Jewish heritage and training was aware of her God's watchful care. But she was unaware of the significance of her life while she waited in the palace. A dramatic journey awaited her.

Our own lives are also involved in a drama that involves the ultimate battle of the ages, in which the Church, the Bride of Christ, plays a leading role alongside her King. He will vanquish every enemy in our lives and in the nations.

So how do we prepare to enter the Lord's presence daily, and prepare for our great wedding day with Him? Surely the King has a chamber protocol that we must present ourselves in.

Just like Esther prepared to meet the king, we are now in a preparation time as the Bride of Christ. We have the Holy Spirit guiding us, comforting us, refining us, and leading us, similar to how Hegai led Esther in her purification process.

Even the oils are symbolic of the process of transformation that we are in now. For six months, Esther was treated with the oil of myrrh, a spice commonly used for preparing bodies for burial. We must die to ourselves and let God reign in us. Death is the first step in preparation for those who will become the Bride of Christ.

"…Count yourselves dead to sin but alive to God in Christ Jesus. Therefore do not let sin reign in your mortal body so that you obey its evil desires. Do not offer the parts of your body to sin, as instruments of wickedness, but rather offer yourselves to God, as those who have been brought from death to life; and offer the parts of your body to Him as instruments of righteousness" (Romans 6:11-13).

This beautification process takes time as our own selfish desires are conformed into His image. Suffering can soften our hard outer shell, so our heavenly Designer can mold and shape us into His perfect image. In Turkey, I learned about how a potter shapes the clay into his own perfect design (Isaiah 45:9), often heating the clay and refashioning it until it fits his image. As I got to make my own design, I saw more of the complex process, and I also got to share with the potter about our Master Designer.

Esther was also in a time of molding, as she willingly entrusted herself to Hegai's care. Whether it was invigorating massages using oil perfumes or exotic makeovers with cosmetics, her one goal was to become more desirable for the king.

Essential oils are symbolic of the Holy Spirit's anointing in our lives to prepare us as Christ's beautiful Bride. The fruit of the Spirit (love, joy, peace, patience, kindness, goodness, faithfulness, gentleness and self-control – Galatians 5:22-23) is being produced in our lives until the day we meet our Bridegroom face to face.

The Lord Himself tells how He bathes and anoints His bride Israel with oil:

"Then I washed thee with water; yea I thoroughly washed away thy blood from thee and I anointed thee with oil" (Ezekiel 16:9, King James Version).

After the extensive treatments in her private chamber, Esther's time came to go to the king. She demonstrated her submissive spirit, by allowing Hegai to choose what she should wear or take with her. This is similar to the way we can trust God's

Holy Spirit. From the moment we receive Christ, the Holy Spirit lives inside us and guides us. Sometimes our own stubborn will interferes, but the Holy Spirit's voice continues to prompt us.

In the movie "The Princess Diaries," a high school student in San Francisco suddenly finds out she is royalty. Instantly, everything changes. Mia now has to step into the role of a princess, and changes have to be made. Her grandmother becomes her instructor on things like beauty, poise and royal protocol. Her grandmother knows more about what it was like to be royalty, so Mia trusts her, even though sometimes she doesn't want to act the way she is instructed.

Belonging to my Bridegroom has defined many of my choices, and I have learned, sometimes regretfully, what influences can tarnish my purity of devotion. I've had to say no to some movies, books, alcohol and other worldly influences that would dilute my focus on Jesus. Each of these choices has come with a price, maybe losing a chance to be with some friends, or denying myself something appealing. But the greater price would be losing the fire of my love for Jesus.

My decisions are not really about saying "no" to things, but instead they are about saying "yes" to wanting all of Jesus. He promises to meet our deepest needs, and as we delight in Him, He promises to give us the desires of our hearts (Psalm 37:4).

Whenever you're struggling with giving things over to God, be honest about your desires, then consciously entrust them to the Lover of your soul to keep and satisfy you in His way and His timing. The more we allow Jesus to fill the empty places in our hearts, the more He can fill us with His joy.

"Blessed are those who have learned to acclaim you, who walk in the light of your presence, O Lord. They rejoice in your name all day long; they exult in your righteousness. For you are their glory and strength, and by your favor you exalt our horn" (Psalm 89:15-17).

Spending time in His presence deepens our love relationship. When I turned 30, I established a new tradition of taking a yearly retreat, a honeymoon with the Lord. It's been amazing to see how the Lord seems to delight in my desire to do this and has provided some amazing surprises for me each year. I love to "get away" to seek Jesus and be in His presence whenever possible.

Finding a place with a conducive environment and no distractions is key. I've been to parks, monasteries, mountains, quiet cafés, chapels, beaches and even secret rooms. I treasure my moments alone with Jesus.

Our set-apart times with Jesus are preparing us to anticipate one day meeting Him face to face. They also prepare us and refine us to be more like Jesus, so others are affected as well.

Esther, through her preparation process, won the favor of everyone who saw her. The night finally came when she went before the king. She must have been so nervous, but one gaze at Esther, and the king was smitten! He chose her to be his queen, and placed a royal crown on her head.

Our Bridegroom King desires that we know Him intimately and experience all of who He is. "One thing I ask of the Lord, this is what I seek: that I may dwell in the house of the Lord all the days of my life, to gaze upon the beauty of the Lord and to seek Him in His temple" (Psalm 27:4). Just as an earthly bride is focused on her bridegroom, Jesus wants us to be focused on Him.

I am such a romantic at heart, and I love to watch a bride walk down the aisle held in the gaze of her Bridegroom. Their deep gaze at the wedding is only a glimpse of the intimacy they will share over a lifetime together. As the Bride of Jesus, our highest calling is simply to be with Him, and pursue Him with all our hearts.

As we come before Him with an undivided heart, we bring a blessing to our Bridegroom. There is a special joy in being with the Lord when no one is watching. I can shut my door and simply worship my King. I can dance, cry or just be silent. The Lord only wants me to be myself, to come before Him without any barriers.

And when we leave His throne room and go back into the world, with all its problems, we carry the Lord's presence with us. We are changed by His love.

Personal Reflection

- What chamber protocol is God calling you to practice? Does your example bring joy and gladness so that others want to enter the palace with you?
- Take some time to praise the Lord for choosing you.
- Petition Him for the requests on your heart, and His heart.

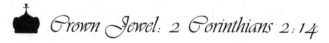

Crown Jewel: 2 Corinthians 2:14

"But thanks be to God, who always leads us in triumphal procession in Christ and through us spreads everywhere the fragrance of the knowledge of him."

Fresh Surrender

I lay my life before You,
A surrendered heart made new;
Fresh revelations of Your Kingship,
Demands choosing Your Lordship;
You are my King of Glory,
Author of our love story;
My dedication seems so small,
To the Holy One who deserves my all!
You alone shall have my soul,
Body and spirit made whole;
In You I find my reason to live,
All of me to You I give.
Take my heart and purify,
Cleanse my sin as I die;
Allowing new life to flow,
Beauty and grace will grow;
At Your right hand are pleasures,
Eye has not seen all your treasures;
My Holy Bridegroom I adore,
Please reveal so much more!
I live to know You and proclaim,
The beauty and splendor of Your fame;
May my life bring You delight,
Until I'm ravished by Your sight!

NW
~ July 29, 2003, Springfield, Missouri ~

Chapter 8

Cultivating Intimacy

"They are led in with joy and gladness;
they enter the palace of the king."

Psalm 45:15

When I was in college, I couldn't get my eating disorder under control, and I didn't understand why. I had become a Christian and gotten rid of so many of the other things in my life that blocked my relationship with God. But this secret sin continued to haunt me.

Then, at my first Christian retreat, I met a girl named Vicki. We hit it off, and I felt the Holy Spirit nudging me to confide in her about my eating disorder. But I was scared. What would she think of me? What would she say?

Then I took a risk. I told her about it, and waited for her response. To my surprise, she confessed struggling with the same problem, and we were able to have a great conversation. It was the first step on the long road to healing.

My main obstacle had been not giving my problem completely to God. I was still holding back, afraid to tell anyone. But God desires us first for Himself, for His presence. We belong to Him.

When we embrace our pain or struggle instead of resisting it or denying it, we allow the Lord to reveal more of His intimate care for us. Life is filled with winds of adversity and blessing, joy and sadness, disappointment and delightful surprises.

Even the confusing, difficult parts of our journey with the King can result in further fruitfulness. Often our pain becomes our platform. My journey in dealing with the roots of my eating disorder in high school and college took me through some painful paths. Facing the truth about our sin can be heart wrenching, but choosing the path of freedom compels us to cast off false security systems to which we have become accustomed.

Sometimes our emotions can be overwhelming, but, in my case, I have had to learn to embrace my feelings and emotions instead of stuffing them down. Inviting the Holy Spirit into every nook and cranny of my heart and life has opened the way to experience true intimacy with Jesus.

In each situation, we can draw closer to our Bridegroom as He conforms us more to His own image. Safely in His love, the Bride of Christ is free to say: "Awake, north wind, and come, south wind! Blow on my garden, that its fragrance may spread abroad..." (Song of Songs 4:16).

The north wind can be harsh or bitter. When life seems to strip us raw, when we experience deep loss, disappointment or hurt. My dad and I are slowly losing my mother to Alzheimer's and it has been a painful process for all of our family. I still cherish seeing her whenever possible. Knowing she is carried in the Good Shepherd's arms, close to His heart (Isaiah 40:11), has comforted me.

When I was particularly sad one day before Christmas, reminiscing on the treasure Mom is to all of us, and missing her so much, the Lord gently spoke to me. Through my tears, I heard His voice whisper softly, "Your mother is body, soul and spirit. Though her outer body is deteriorating, her inner spirit is being renewed day by day" (2 Corinthians 4:16).

Though I had heard this promise before, it now had new personal meaning to me. Often as I care for my mother, I communicate with her spirit to spirit, knowing she is in direct communication with the Lord through her spirit. We have a precious relationship that transcends her earthly condition.

But even as I anticipate having to say goodbye to my mother and father on this earth, the Lord gave me another promise in the midst of my tears one day. "Though my father and mother forsake me, the Lord will receive me" (Psalm 27:10). The Lord will always be there for us, in every season of life, both in loss and blessing.

In contrast to the north winds of our lives, the south wind is warm and inviting, and we can experience His gentle love and goodness in comforting ways. The Spirit blows on our garden so that its fragrance will spread all over the world. The Lord invites us to share all our experiences with Him, good and bad, because each one deepens our intimacy with Him.

Cultivating intimacy with Jesus is similar to a human relationship, yet goes far beyond the depths we understand. For any relationship to flourish and become intimate, priority focus must be given to it. It must surpass all other loves to captivate your heart and consume your emotions.

Worshipping Jesus in the splendor of His holiness deepens our intimacy. The word "worship" comes from proskuneo, which means to "kiss toward." When we worship, we come face to face, spirit to spirit, with our Bridegroom. "The Lord confides in those who fear Him; He makes His covenant known to them" (Psalm 25:14).

Our heavenly Bridegroom also blesses us with His intimate presence. I often whisper to Jesus, "I need a kiss today," echoing the cry of the Beloved in Song of Songs 1:1-4, wishing for some special blessing from the Lord. I've been amazed at some of His tender expressions of love.

One Valentine's Day, when I was attending a friend's wedding, I felt the need for some encouragement from the Lord. So I prayed for something special, a kiss from God. I wasn't bemoaning, I just wanted an expression from the Lord. I came home that day and found three red roses sitting in a vase at my front door. I still don't know who they were from, but I know it was my Bridegroom's special way of surprising me.

More recently, I needed a time of renewal with the Lord, so I prayed for a special blessing, and wow, did God bless me! Through the generosity of some friends, I was invited to Hawaii! The Lord knew that of all the places in the world that I could go, Hawaii would bless me the most. It's not always an exotic vacation, but the Lord longs to give us our heart's desire. Sometimes I have been blessed through human encouragement or when a Scripture comes to mind, renewing my spirit.

God has given us so many love letters in His precious Word, declaring His intentions toward us, and describing His incomparable covenant love for us. I often carry His Word on index cards to meditate on and hide in my heart. Memorizing His Word allows it to come quickly to our minds in the midst of our needs.

Our Beloved speaks to us through His Word, and we can sift our thoughts by the confirmation of His Word. Jesus said: "My sheep listen to my voice; I know them, and they follow me" (John 10:27).

Hearing God's voice takes time and quiet. Listening must be cultivated, especially in our noisy world. We are daily bombarded with external and internal voices that seek to rob us of hearing His voice.

God's voice will always agree with His Word and will never contradict it. It may be convicting but won't be condemning. God's voice may sound like yours, but His Spirit will initiate it. It can be a still, small voice or it may be strong and clear. I've made it my habit to take time to spend with my Beloved, listening to Him, communicating with Him through worship and prayer, meditating and studying His Word.

But being a Type A personality with lots of energy and ideas keeps me busy, and I have a constant danger to crowd out the ability to hear my Lord's voice. During one particular season, my life had been very exciting, filled with lots of ministry opportunities, speaking about Jesus, and planning future mission trips. But I managed to get away for a day with my King, and I felt Jesus desiring more of me for Himself. As I listened attentively that peaceful day, He spoke to me: "This is what the Sovereign Lord, the Holy One of Israel, says: 'In repentance and rest is your salvation, in quietness and trust is your strength, but you would have none of it'" (Isaiah 30:15).

God's Spirit gently urged me to repent of my busyness and tendency to want others' approval at the risk of compromising my love and devotion to Him. As I cried tears of sadness for my human weakness, He forgave me and gave me a fresh promise: "Yet the Lord longs to be gracious to you; He rises to show you compassion. For the Lord is a God of justice. Blessed are all who wait for Him" (Isaiah 30:18).

Our Lord is so gracious. He delights in those who wait for Him. He assured me of His leadership in my life, that I was His sheep and He was my Shepherd. I didn't have to figure out every step on my own, but simply rest in Him and trust that He would guide me step by step. "Whether you turn to the right or to the left, your ears will hear a voice behind you, saying, 'This is the way; walk in it'" (Isaiah 30:21).

As you consider cultivating your intimacy with Your heavenly Bridegroom, ask Him to draw you and woo you with His intimate love. He is pursuing your heart and desires more of you. Your relationship with Him can be exciting and intimate. "Arise, my darling, my beautiful one, and come with Me" (Song of Songs 2:10).

Personal Reflection

- When do you feel closest to God?
- What barriers do you have in your life that block your intimacy with God?
- What are the good and bad areas of your life that God wants you to share with Him?

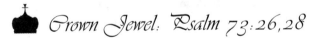

Crown Jewel: Psalm 73:26,28

"My flesh and my heart my fail,
but God is the strength of my heart and my portion forever…
But as for me, it is good to be near God.
I have made the Sovereign Lord my refuge;
I will tell of all your deeds."

Come Up Higher, My Beloved

Though the journey may seem steep, There are bountiful joys to reap;
Perilous paths will be crossed, Safe with me, nothing is lost;
You only must travel light, To arrive at the magnificent sight;
Fears and doubts will come your way, That's when you need to pray!
I give my angels charge over you, My promises all prove true!
When tempted to feel alone, My intimate presence is shone;
Oh, the glory I want to show, Those who fear me will know;
Take my hand and come higher, My love,
Beauty and revelation come from above;
Eye has not seen, nor ear heard, All that is prepared from My Word!
See the eagle fly, So high in the sky;
I long for you to soar, Let your heart adore!
My Beloved Bride so free, You were made for Me!
My arms are open wide, Calling them to your side.

NW
Received from my Beloved after climbing to the top
of an overlook of the Arkansas River
August 22, 2005

The *Kingdom*

"…You are worthy to take the scroll and to open its seals, because you were slain, and with your blood you purchased men for God from every tribe and language and people and nation. You have made them to be a kingdom and priests to serve our God, and they will reign on the earth."

Revelation 5:9-10

Chapter 9

Commissioned by the King

"Your sons will take the place of your fathers;
you will make them princes throughout the land.."

Psalm 45:16

When Jesus began His ministry, the Jewish people who believed He was the Messiah expected Him to begin a new kingdom. They assumed He would overthrow the Roman rule and set His kingdom in power. When He didn't do things the way the thought He would, they brought Him before Pilate, and accused Him of claiming to be king.

"Are you the king of the Jews?" Pilate asked him.

"Is this your own idea," Jesus asked, "or did others talk to you about me? … My kingdom is not of this world. If it were, my servants would fight to prevent my arrest by the Jews. But now my kingdom is from another place" (John 18:33, 34, 36).

Jesus didn't come to set up an earthly kingdom, but instead He came to usher in a different kind of kingdom—a kingdom of the heart.

As the Bride of Jesus Christ, we are one with Him in all His kingdom purposes. At a friend's wedding shower, someone commented, "Now that she's getting married, she will get more involved in her husband's world." I smiled, thinking, *Yes, and my husband (Jesus) owns the whole world, so I will go with Him!*

Whether you are single, married or divorced, if you are the Bride of Jesus, you also have become a battling Bride. Our Bridegroom is engaged in serious Kingdom business. Just as a wife shares her husband's concerns, so we are united with Christ in overcoming the evil forces of Satan.

In Esther's story, she was intimately united with the king, the most powerful man in the world at that time. But when a decree came that all the Jews were to be killed, she decided to risk everything she had been given, even her life, to go before the king and ask him to spare her people. Mordecai warned her:

"For if you remain silent at this time, relief and deliverance for the Jews will arise from another place, but you and your father's family will perish. And who knows but that you have come to royal position for such a time as this?" (Esther 4:14).

If she had not been confident in her God, she could not have been courageous enough to embrace her destiny and risk everything to save her people. When faced with this critical choice, Esther chose to trust in her God and live up to her royal status. Though she didn't choose her position, she came to realize that her royal authority was "for such a time as this."

Her calling became crystal clear to her, in light of the crisis of her Jewish people.

She was intricately involved in the cosmic battle of the ages between two kingdoms, God's and Satan's, as Satan tried to wipe out God's people.

The battle continues to this day and as the Bride of the Messiah, we can pray and stand with God's chosen people and to reach the rest of the world with His great love.

The first of my yearly retreats with Jesus was to Israel, where I studied with a group of Jewish people who all believed in Jesus, called Messianic Jews. The Bible came alive to me in a whole new way, as I began to study the parallels between the Jewish customs and traditions in the Old Testament and Jesus' fulfillment of all of them.

I fell in love with Israel and have been back several times to pray for both the Jewish and Arabic people.

One day I was hoping to find a specific ring I had heard was sold in a few shops. I stepped into one shop in the Old City of Jerusalem, and found out the owner's name was Esther.

Reminiscing of my study of Esther's story in the Bible, I asked her whether or not she knew the significance of her name.

I told her, "Esther is my heroine, because she boldly went before the King, after fasting for three days and three nights, risking her life, deciding, 'If I perish, I perish'" (Esther 4:16).

This woman listened attentively to me, a non-Jew, as I praised her namesake. We connected heart to heart. I went on recounting the story. "My favorite part is the moment the king saw Esther standing in the court. She must have looked so regal, so elegant, so courageous. He favored her again by extending the golden scepter, the symbol of his power and authority. She then came near and touched the top of the scepter, embracing the authority he was bestowing upon her. The next part blows my mind. 'Then the king asked, "What is it, Queen Esther? What is your request? Even up to half the kingdom, it will be given you"'" (Esther 5:3).

I couldn't resist exclaiming, "Oh, Esther, it's so exciting how God then used Esther to save her people from destruction. She understood the power and authority entrusted to her and boldly used it, not for selfish gain, but for changing history forever.

"Esther, have you ever considered that Jesus could be the promised Messiah that your people are waiting for, that history really is His story?"

I waited for her response, as she was silent, then she smiled softly. "I don't know," she whispered. "Well, I do," I gently whispered back. "Yeshua HaMashiach (the Hebrew name for Jesus the Messiah) is God's promised Messiah, and He loves you, Esther, and gave His life so you could be His Bride forever.

"I will pray He opens your eyes and heart to understand who Yeshua really is," I told her. Then I asked her about the reason I came to her store. "Do you have any silver rings that have 'I am my Beloved's and He is mine' engraved in Hebrew?" I asked. It was a fairly common ring, taken from Song of Songs 2:16, but I hadn't been able to find one yet. Esther reached into the glass shelf, then gently lifted my left hand and slipped the most delicate, beautiful silver ring, on my left finger.

It took my breath away. Jesus had given me a symbol of His love, at the same time that I was able to share that love with the very person selling me the ring.

Queen Esther, along with other men and women of God, make up the Bridal host of believers through the ages who made a mark on their generation. Our Bridegroom is inviting each of us in our generation to take our place in history and help increase His kingdom.

I have an old tattered map that I use to pray for lost people around the world, and I sometimes light a candle and pray over it. The Lord has blessed those times, and often directed me to go to the countries I've prayed for. "Be careful what you pray," I've often heard, "you may become the answer." Pray dangerously and obey expectantly!

Recently, I read some news reports about young children in the Middle East being trained as suicide bombers. I prayed for all the young people in the world, and I asked the Lord where to focus my prayers. He gave me a burden for Turkey, a large country north of Israel with a rich culture, and I was soon given an opportunity to visit there.

In Istanbul, my friends and I visited a famous blue mosque, with a desire to go and pray there. We asked to enter, but were denied.

"You are not Muslim," the man at the door said.

"Oh, but we have come to pray for your country," I responded. "Don't you think that is a good idea?"

He thought for a moment and said, "OK, but put on this headscarf first."

Taking off our shoes and donning our blue headscarves gave us the right of passage. We knelt down in the women's section, and as I listened to the Iman chanting prayers and seeing the people bow down to a false god, my heart was grieved. I opened my Bible to Psalm 24, and the Holy Spirit spoke to my heart. "The King of glory has come into this place. He lives inside of you, Nancy!" I rejoiced at this revelation, and then the Holy Spirit led me to this promise for Turkey: "All the ends of the earth will remember and turn to the Lord, and all the families of the nations will bow down before Him, for dominion belongs to the Lord and He rules over the nations" (Psalm 22:27-28).

While I was praising His victory and declaring His Word

(silently of course), a veiled woman, covered from head to foot in black, came over and patted my head, as if to say, "Good little religious girl." I smiled broadly and hugged her, whispering in her ear, "Isa (the Arabic pronunciation of Jesus) loves you!" Since she didn't speak English, I could only trust the Spirit of God to reach into this precious woman's heart.

My love for the Turkish people continued to grow, especially as I encountered such openness from the young people and the women. Gradually, through relationships, God opened opportunities and divine appointments, but my heart went out to the whole nation. I began to pray Isaiah 60:1-3, specifically for Turkey. I placed the country name into the verse, and prayed like this:

Arise, shine, for your light has come, Turkey,
and the glory of the Lord rises upon Turkey.
See darkness covers the earth and thick darkness over the
    Turkish peoples,
but the Lord rises upon you, Turkey,
and his glory appears over you, Turkish people.
Nations will come to the light of Turkey,
And kings to the brightness of the Turkish dawn.

I'd been praying this for about a week, when one of my friends introduced me to Mustafa, a man who runs a Christian radio station. His story is an amazing testimony of God reaching a religious Muslim. He has faced many challenges, but like a modern day apostle Paul, he boldly faces opposition with courage and faith in the Lord. He invited me to be his guest on his hour and a half radio talk show. Approximately 35 million people could potentially listen. Because it was an officially approved station, I could freely share the gospel. I was blown away with the way the Lord answered my prayer to preach the gospel to more of the Turkish people. But why should I be amazed? His character is to seek and save the lost (Luke 19:10).

I was overwhelmed with the number of women who called in to the show. Apparently, they were connecting with my life, and several called after the show. One asked if my books were translated into Turkish. Mustafa responded, "No, but we will do it!" I gasped, "Oh my, how does this happen?" He said he could provide translation and publishing if I could provide the money.

We committed it to the Lord, knowing that if it was His will, He would provide all that was needed. The next day, I was invited to another radio station to tape two programs, each an hour long. Again, God did far more than I would have even thought to ask. My awesome Bridegroom King gave me the privilege to represent Him over the airwaves of Turkey, and miraculously has already provided the money to publish "In Pursuit of the Ideal" in Turkish, due to the gracious generosity of some faith-filled friends.

There's simply no limit to what the all-consuming love of Jesus will do. His fiery love burns through any barrier and opens doors no man can shut (Revelation 3:7). And there are so many divine opportunities that He doesn't want us to miss. During my time in Hawaii, I was praying for the Middle East when I caught the accent of the family taking a picture near me. As I offered to take the picture for them, I found out they were from Iran, and I told them I had just been praying for the Middle East. "Please continue to pray for us!" they said. I promised that I would. I invite you each to join me in praying that God will freshly anoint His Bride to fulfill His purposes.

Personal Reflection

- What situation might God have placed you in "for such a time as this?" How would He want to act?
- Ask God to enlarge your vision for the world. What nation is He placing on your heart to pray for? To give money for missions? To go yourself?
- What risks is God asking you to take to increase His Kingdom?

Crown Jewel: Psalm 2:8

"Ask of me, and I will make the nations your inheritance,
the ends of the earth your possession."

Your Signet Ring

"Place me like a seal over Your heart,"
You captured my love from the start;
Like a seal on Your arm, Protected from all harm;
Love burns like blazing fire, A mighty flame of desire;
Many waters cannot quench love, Pure as a spotless dove;
Jealous love is strong, Willing to confront wrong;
Haggai listened for Your Word, Powerful as a sharp sword;
A royal crown Esther wore, Mordecai was given more;
The signet ring from the King, His authority it would bring;
Zerubbabel heard "On that day," Declares the Lord Almighty;
"I will make you like My signet ring, For I have chosen you for this thing!"
As the hour of evil encroaches, The day of destiny approaches;
Help me embrace my role, To be a pure bridal soul;
Anointed and waiting, Listening, obeying;
Wearing Your signet ring, Victory and praise I'll bring.

NW
~ March 20, 2004 ~

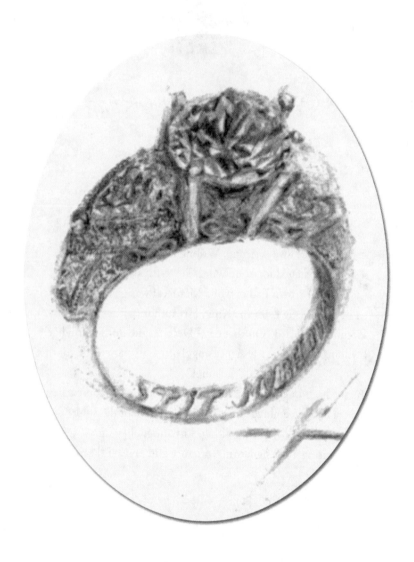

Chapter 10

Covenant-Keeping King

*"I will perpetuate your memory
through all generations…"*

Psalm 45:17

In a Jewish bridal tradition, the covenant of marriage was established at the time of the engagement. Parents often arranged the marriages, but the bride and bridegroom each gave consent. The prospective bridegroom would go the bride's house for a special meal, and after the dinner, he would lift a cup of wine called the kiddush (sanctification) cup and say, "Blessed art Thou, O Lord, Our God, King of the universe, Creator of the fruit of the vine."

He would then hand it to the bride, and if she drank from the cup, she showed her willingness to enter this union by saying "yes" to his proposal. After sharing the cup of wine, they entered into a binding relationship, one that required a legal transaction to break the agreement. Their shared cup of wine, called B'rit (covenant), symbolized the sealing of their marriage covenant in blood. The engaged couple, for all legal purposes, was married.

Similarly, Jesus, our Bridegroom has made a covenant with us. He told His disciples at the last Passover He celebrated with them, "…This cup is the new covenant in my blood, which is poured out for you" (Luke 22:20).

Covenants are not talked about commonly anymore. We are most familiar with the marriage covenant, where a man and woman pledge themselves to each other "for better or for worse, till death do us part." Although it is meant to be a permanent binding relationship, it is often broken by the fallibility of human love.

But our divine Lover shows us His perfect flawless, amazing, sacrificial love in His total giving of Himself. Every bride longs for the extravagant love of her bridegroom pledging himself to her. We can rejoice in God's covenant with us, as we seek to tell others about His glorious commitment to His Bride.

If we were to trace back to when the Lord chose Israel as a nation to display His glory and purposes, we would see His covenant woven throughout His communication with His people. Can you imagine the pain of our Bridegroom King when He pursued Israel with such intensity and faithfulness, only to have her forsake Him time and time again?

Just look at the book of Jeremiah. It is a continual journey of the way God sought after His people, yet they turned away again and again. The words of the prophet have gripped my heart with the heart of God for His people. He warns them, calls out to them, pursues them and asks questions of them. But the overwhelming response He receives is rejection. "This is what the Lord says: 'Stand at the crossroads and look; ask for the ancient paths, ask where the good way is, and walk in it, and you will find rest for your souls.' But you said, 'We will not walk in it' " (Jeremiah 6:16-17).

We are so often like the children of Israel, stubborn in our ways. The Lord continues to give promises to them if they will choose Him and listen to His words. In order to truly grasp the magnitude of this unconditional love, we must understand the test of our King's love – that in the face of rejection He continues to pursue His Beloved.

My heart continually goes out to the people of God's first covenant, the Jews. He continues to seek them after thousands of years. Sadly, many have been wounded deeply, even killed in the name of "Christianity." There is a great need for healing and reconciliation between believers in "Yeshua" and the Jewish people. As I have begun to understand this more thoroughly, my heart has been broken at how our Lord Jesus has been misrepresented to them.

As the Bride of Christ, we can bring His love to them, if we are willing to humble ourselves and repent of the atrocities they have incurred over history. We are uniting with our Shepherd Bridegroom when we do so.

"For this is what the Sovereign Lord says: I myself will search for my sheep and look after them. As a shepherd looks after his scattered flock when he is with them, so will I look after my sheep. I will rescue them from all the places where they were scattered on a day of clouds and darkness" (Ezekiel 34:11-12).

One of my favorite places to visit is called Canaan in the Desert, in Phoenix, Arizona. It is the U.S. branch of the Evangelical Sisterhood of Mary, a worldwide community born out of the ruins of World War II in Germany. Their ministry is primarily focused on repentance toward the Jewish people, and rekindling first love for Jesus in these end-times. The sisters have become dear friends and partners in prayer. Several times a year I go there to seek the Lord, write and be refreshed in His presence.

Recently, while visiting Canaan, I met an elderly Jewish woman named Esther. She is a Holocaust survivor, along with only two other family members out of ten. From the age of 9 to 16 years, she suffered immeasurable pain and witnessed many horrors. Her memories have plagued her all these years, and her only son cares for her in her growing dementia. I can't begin to imagine all she has been through, but it was a privilege to pray with her and extend Jesus' love to her.

I caught a glimpse of God's heart for Esther and her people. Ezekiel's words came alive to me: "I will search for the lost and bring back the strays. I will bind up the injured and strengthen the weak" (Ezekiel 34:16).

Even though many of the Jewish people still don't recognize Jesus as their Messiah, He is committed to them in covenant love. Despite all the suffering and rejection of the Jewish people throughout history, our Savior's love has not diminished.

As we see Israel's choice of other gods throughout the Bible, may we recognize our own tendency to choose other loves, and depart from the Lover of our souls.

None of us deserves this covenant love, but the prophet Jeremiah tells of an even greater blessing. "'For I know the plans I have for you,' declares the Lord, 'plans to prosper you and not to harm you, plans to give you hope and a future'" (Jeremiah 29:11).

These often-quoted words of promise bring hope to each one of us, as well as to the nations. The Lord wants us to know His covenant love. There is great promise for Israel and each Bridal soul who embraces His covenant love.

Jeremiah was foretelling the new covenant that would be made by our Bridegroom King with His chosen Bride. "'The time is coming,' declares the Lord, 'when I will make a new covenant with the house of Israel and with the house of Judah. It will not be like the covenant I made with their forefathers when I took them by the hand to lead them out of Egypt, because they broke my covenant, though I was a husband to them,' declares the Lord" (Jeremiah 31:31-32).

Our covenant-keeping King has made a NEW covenant that He initiated out of love and longing for us. He sent His own beloved Son, Jesus Christ, to complete the covenant for us. "For this reason Christ is the mediator of a new covenant, that those who are called may receive the promised eternal inheritance—now that He has died as a ransom to set them free from the sins committed under the first covenant" (Hebrews 9:15).

At the end of our time on earth, there will be a "happily ever after" with our Prince and King, to rule and reign with Him forever. This is truly the essence and goal of His story, to claim His beloved Bride.

Personal Reflection

- How would you explain a covenant?
- How does it make you feel to be in a covenant?
- Is there a specific people group you are reaching out to?
  Take some time to pray about where God might be leading you.

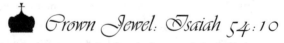

Crown Jewel: Isaiah 54:10

"'Though the mountains be shaken and the hills be removed,
yet my unfailing love for you will not be shaken
nor my covenant of peace be removed,'
says the Lord, who has compassion on you."

Yeshua, My Love

Your name is like perfume poured out,
Your love is something to sing about!
More delightful than wine,
With you I choose to dine;
You have taken me away,
What a beautiful day;
Your intimate presence warms me,
Revealing Your passionate plea;
"Come with Me, My Bride,"
Abide with Me, at my side;
You have stolen my heart
with one glance of your eyes,"
"You are a garden fountain, a well of flowing water,"
My heart sighs…
Let my lover come and taste,
Not a minute to waste;
Blow on my garden with gentle breeze,
Every opportunity I'll seize;
To let Your fragrance spread
With Your hand I'm led.

NW
~ August 30, 2003, Zurich, Switzerland ~

Chapter 11

Consuming Love

"...Therefore the nations will praise you..."
Psalm 45:17

Since I was a little girl, I prayed for Africa, and felt some day I would go to tell the people about Jesus. Over half of the population is under 18, and 25 million Africans are infected with AIDS, resulting in millions of orphans.

In 2001, "Operation Sunrise Africa" was launched by Campus Crusade for Christ in Southern and Eastern Africa, using Malachi 4:2 as the theme: "But for you who revere My name, the sun of righteousness will rise with healing in its wings. And you will go out and leap like calves released from the stall." The strategy was to reach 50 million people in 50 cities in 50 days with the gospel.

As an International Ambassador of Student Venture, (the junior high and high school outreach of Campus Crusade) I wanted to go and help mobilize teams of college and high school students. God honors faith, so I began to pray, "Lord, show me Your glory like never before." My joy was to co-lead a team to Uganda, a nation formerly ravaged by tyrant Idi Amin, who killed over 300,000 Ugandans and foreigners.

In just 12 days, we preached the gospel in 30 high school assemblies, and over 5,000 people indicated decisions to accept Christ. I can't begin to describe the overwhelming joy I felt when nine Muslim boys came forward to give their hearts to Christ.

They risked the rejection of family and even possible death. They were instructed by the local believers in their new faith and are being taught how to grow in Christ. When they are stronger, they can begin to share their faith as He leads.

After Operation Sunrise, Student Venture launched a high school ministry in Nairobi, Kenya, where a model is being raised up for other African nations. I just returned this summer from my fourth mission to this beautiful nation. After training 350 young leaders and going with some of them to reach their high schools, I know God is truly raising up a new generation of young believers in Africa and all over the world.

While there, I visited the Tumaini Children's Home in Nakuru, Kenya, which houses 28 children who have been rescued from the streets. Before coming to the home, most of the children were barely surviving, eating from garbage dumps to fill their stomachs and addicted to the easy high from epoxy (glue) to try and fill the void in their lives. Many had lost their parents to AIDS. Several couples in Kenya had set up feeding stations in the streets for the orphans, and then they would lead the children to Jesus and adopt them.

The children I met are the first fruits of a new ministry birthed out of God's consuming love for "the least of these" (Matthew 25:40). What excited me the most was the way the children were being loved and equipped to go out and minister to other street kids.

"Do not be afraid, for I am with you; I will bring your children from the east and gather you from the west. I will say to the north, 'Give them up!' and to the south, 'Do not hold them back.' Bring my sons from afar and my daughters from the ends of the earth—everyone who is called by my name, whom I created for my glory, whom I formed and made'" (Isaiah 43:5-7).

This passage has gripped me as I've caught a big picture of my King's awesome heart for His children all over the world. Each one is formed by Him and created for His glory. I've carried each one of the Nakuru children in my heart, as well as children I met in Uganda, and I'm trusting that God will bring sponsors for each one of them. (If you are interested in sponsoring a child or supporting some national youth workers, see page

150, "Opportunities for the Bride"). The workers and students in Kenya, Uganda and throughout the world are my young heroes, making a difference in their generations.

Just above Kenya lies a very difficult part of the world, often called "the 10/40 Window." It is a section of the world considered the least touched by the gospel. It roughly spans from 10 degrees latitude to 40 degrees latitude north, and stretches from West Africa to East Asia. Almost two thirds of the world's people (3.6 billion) live in the 10/40 Window. Within this area are 2 billion people who have never heard of Jesus as Savior and are not within reach of Christians among their own people. They haven't rejected Him—they have never had an opportunity to hear the gospel.

DID YOU KNOW?

- 94 percent of the people living in the 65 least-evangelized countries also live in the 10/40 Window.
- 79 percent of the world's poorest also live in the least-evangelized countries of the world.
- 2/3 of the world's population has an oral preference (can't or won't read and write)
- 5,000 people groups are not yet reached with the gospel
- 2,700 remaining people groups are Bibleless

Four Major Religious Blocks in the 10/40 Window (shaded area)

3.6 billion unreached people

- Muslims   880 Million   24%
- Hindu   800 Million   23%
- Buddhist   230 Million   6%
- Non-Religious 700 Million   20%

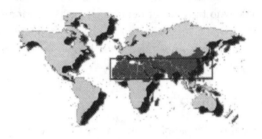

(sources: http://epic.ccci.org/epc/Our_Vision.htm, Morris Cerullo World Evangelism)

According to Window International Network, a ministry that exists to help reach the 10/40 Window, "Many of these 10/40 Window nations lack religious freedom. Christian Believers in these nations are intimidated, raped, harassed, tortured, pressured to renounce their faith, discriminated against, denied health care, education, and jobs, starved, and even murdered for worshipping the one, true God. It is a horrifying reality that more Christians were killed for their faith in the 20th century than in all the previous centuries combined. The largest group of people being persecuted for their faith in the world today is Christians" (Praying Through the Window 8 prayer calendar).

Over half of these unheard voices are women – wives, mothers and daughters. Over a billion people have never even heard the gospel. We need to join with our sisters in Christ in the persecuted church and lift them up in prayer. "We are hard pressed on every side, but not crushed; perplexed, but not in despair; persecuted, but not abandoned, struck down, but not destroyed" (2 Corinthians 4:8-9). We need to take bold steps of faith if we are to see the light of the gospel penetrate the darkest corners of the earth. My personal life passage is Isaiah 61, The Year of the Lord's Favor. Stop for a minute and meditate on this passage. Could it be true of you?

"The Spirit of the Sovereign Lord is on me, because the Lord has <u>anointed me to preach good news</u> to the poor.

He has <u>sent me to bind up the brokenhearted</u>,

to <u>proclaim freedom for the captives</u> and release for the prisoners,

to <u>proclaim the year of the Lord's favor</u> and the day of vengeance of our God,

<u>to comfort all who mourn</u>, and <u>provide for those who grieve</u> in Zion—to bestow on them a crown of beauty instead of ashes., the oil of gladness instead of mourning, and a garment of praise instead of a spirit of despair.

"They will be called oaks of righteousness, a planting of the Lord for the display of His splendor" (Isaiah 61:1-3, emphasis mine).

When I traveled to Turkey, my journey began by a prayer expedition to the seven churches mentioned in the book of Revelation. As I learned more about the once thriving church at Ephesus, where Paul was used mightily to bring the gospel, it was more sobering to realize that in Revelation, Christ holds one thing against them: they had left their first love.

No one wants to leave their first love. After all, this is the intoxicating, fiery love that causes people to do extravagant things to demonstrate their love. Have you ever observed an engaged or newly married couple? They are affectionate and eager to be together, often oblivious to others around them. They would choose time with each other rather than anything else.

What keeps first love alive and thriving? I believe it is the result of being loved, both knowing and experiencing it. "We love because He first loved us" (I John 4:19).

Our passionate Lover wants to consume us with Himself. When Moses described God to the people, he said: "For the Lord your God is a consuming fire, a jealous God" (Deuteronomy 4:24). He is jealous for you and desires every part of you to be immersed in His love. God's ravished heart for His Bride is seen all through Song of Songs love affair.

"...for love is as strong as death, its jealousy unyielding as the grave. It burns like blazing fire, like a mighty flame. Many waters cannot quench love; rivers cannot wash it away. If one were to give all the wealth of his house for love, it would be utterly scorned"

(Song of Songs 8:6,7).

The more we allow God to romance our hearts and minds with His consuming love, it will burn through every compromise and every contender for our heart.

The Ephesian church was busy doing good deeds, persevering and enduring evil men, but somehow the relationship of love had taken second place to their work for Him. At times, the busyness of my ministry has threatened to rob me of my first love for Jesus. I'm reminded of what Jesus told the Ephesians: "Remember the height from which you have fallen! Repent and do the things you did at first. If you do not repent, I will come to you and remove your lampstand from its place" (Revelation 2:5).

As I fall at my Lover's feet in repentance, basking in His forgiveness, I renew my heart of intimate love for Him. I'm freshly smitten by His gracious love, the fire is rekindled and as it burns brightly again I can be a flame to stir the hearts of people wherever He leads.

❧ *Personal Reflection* ❧

- Pray that the Lord's all-consuming love would compel you to be His ambassador to this generation.

"For Christ's love compels us, because we are convinced that one died for all, and therefore all died. And He died for all, that those who live should no longer live for themselves but for Him who died for them and was raised again . . . We are therefore Christ's ambassadors, as though God were making His appeal through us. We implore you on Christ's behalf: Be reconciled to God" (2 Corinthians 5:14-15, 20).

- Write down some of the things that fight for your affection.
- Ask God to ignite a fresh passion in you to fulfill His purpose.

♛ *Crown Jewel: Matthew 28:18-20*

Then Jesus came to them and said, "All authority in heaven and on earth has been given to me. Therefore go and make disciples of all nations, baptizing them in the name of the Father and of the Son and of the Holy Spirit, and teaching them to obey everything I have commanded you. And surely I am with you always, to the very end of the age."

Kingdom Vision

Oh, grant me eyes to see
Beyond what affects me;
May I, like Habbakuk, call,
To understand the sum of all;
You and Your eternal plan
Miraculously involves man;
With amazement I look,
Your own Son You forsook;
To give His life for His Bride,
To reign eternally at His side;
Beyond my human mind,
Only through You I find;
Grace to watch and pray
To see what You will say;
I station myself to hear,
Humbly I draw near;
Your revelation I await,
To write and not hesitate;
Faith enables me to run,
Lifting up Your Son;

"For the earth will be filled,
With the knowledge of the glory of the Lord,
As the waters cover the sea,
Let all the earth be stilled,
Before Him . . . the Lord is in His holy temple."
Lord, I have heard of Your fame,
The glory of Your great NAME;
I stand in awe of who You are,
Oh Bright and Morning Star;
Renew Your deeds in our day,
Put Your glory on display;
Splendor as the sunrise,
Let Your power arise!
Ancient mountains crumble
At Your Holy rumble;
Mighty to save Your anointed,
The time is already appointed;
In You, I will wait and rejoice,
You are my precious choice!
Sovereign Lord, strengthen my feet,
On the mountain heights, You I'll meet!

NW
~ March 10, 2004, Bangkok, Thailand ~

Chapter 12

Come Lord Jesus

"...forever and ever."
Psalm 45:17

One morning in Hawaii I woke early, eager to see the sunrise. I walked outside, and there was a stillness, a complete darkness, and no trace of the sun yet. But I knew it would come soon.

As surely as it had set the night before, the last tip of the bright yellow-orange sun slipping into the sea, I knew it would rise again. So I waited in the cool morning quietness, my heart anticipating the beauty that I knew was coming.

As I waited, I felt a longing for more than just the sunrise. There was a deeper longing in my heart, a desire for the Son of righteousness to appear. One day He will come for His Bride and establish His righteous rule. Tears began to stream down my cheeks with the revelation of this truth. My beloved Bridegroom is coming for His Bride and they together will reign and rule forever and ever.

After Jesus rose from the dead, and was seen by many people, He ascended into heaven before the disciples' very eyes. They stood looking intently up into the sky when two men dressed in white stood beside them.

"'Men of Galilee,' they said, 'why do you stand here looking into the sky? This same Jesus, who has been taken from you into heaven, will come back in the same way you have seen Him go into heaven'" (Acts 1:11).

Our victorious Champion, Jesus, has finished His work on the cross, but the end of the course has not yet come. He is coming for His Bride, who has made herself ready, and with her all of history will culminate.

After a Jewish couple would get engaged, the bridegroom went back to his father's house to prepare for the wedding. It would be approximately a year, but the bride didn't know exactly when the wedding would take place. Neither did the bridegroom – his father decided when it was time. So the bride waited at her house until they heard the bridegroom or his groomsmen yell, and the blowing of the shofar, an instrument made of a ram's horn.

Just like the Jewish bride, we as the Bride of Christ are in a period of waiting. Christ Himself used the example of the wedding when He talked about waiting and being prepared. "...The kingdom of heaven will be like ten virgins who took their lamps and went out to meet the bridegroom. Five of them were foolish and five were wise. The foolish ones took their lamps but did not take any oil with them. The wise, however, took oil in jars along with their lamps. The bridegroom was a long time in coming, and they all became drowsy and fell asleep. At midnight the cry rang out: 'Here's the bridegroom! Come out to meet him!' "Then all the virgins woke up and trimmed their lamps. The foolish ones said to the wise, 'Give us some of your oil; our lamps are going out.' 'No,' they replied, 'there may not be enough for both us and you. Instead, go to those who sell oil and buy some for yourselves.' But while they were on their way to buy the oil, the bridegroom arrived. The virgins who were ready went in with him to the wedding banquet. And the door was shut. Later the others also came. 'Sir! Sir!' they said. 'Open the door for us!' But he replied, 'I tell you the truth, I don't know you.' Therefore keep watch, because you do not know the day or the hour" (Matthew 25:1-13).

One day very soon, we will see our Beloved face to face, never to be separated eternally. I get so excited just thinking of this honor. It will take all eternity to grasp the implications of our queenly role, as we rule and reign with Jesus forever. "In My Father's house are many rooms; if it were not so, I would have told you. I am going there to prepare a place for you. And if I go and prepare a place for you, I will come back and take you to be with me that you also may be where I am" (John 14:2-3).

Now we are engaged in the final climactic battle between the kingdom of light and the kingdom of darkness, between all good and evil. The stakes are high, and countless souls are waiting to be rescued. Multitudes are in the valley of decision. In my mind's eye, I see the lost in many of the countries to which I've traveled, and the harvest ripening everywhere.

Studying the book of Joel shed more insight into the future culminating events that the world will face. The Old Testament prophet Joel paints a graphic picture of the "day of the Lord": "The Lord thunders at the head of His army; His forces are beyond number, and mighty are those who obey His command. The day of the Lord is great; it is dreadful. Who can endure it?" (Joel 2:11).

God has prepared everything for His perfect timing. Our role is to keep watch and be ready, "because the Son of Man will come at an hour when you do not expect Him" (Matthew 24:44). Then, far more dramatic than a sunrise, He will come. "For as lightning that comes from the east is visible even in the west, so will be the coming of the Son of Man" (Matthew 24:27).

As the days grow more evil and dark, the light will shine brighter and brighter until the full day. The Bride of Jesus Christ is His beautiful representative in these final days. Now we only see in a mirror dimly, but then we will see face to face (1 Corinthians 13:12). The artist is still putting His final touches on the canvas of our love story.

Our battle now is for the souls of people all around the world. The time is short.

I'll never forget two of my neighbors, a couple named Mike and Helen. Mike was an ex-Marine who had been paralyzed by a stroke and confined to a wheelchair. He had become very bitter, but the Lord gave me such a love and burden for him to know Jesus. I would visit with him, make him laugh, bring him treats, and remind him that one day he could have a new resurrection body (1 Corinthians 15:50-55) if he put his trust in Jesus.

His condition worsened, his leg was amputated, and he stayed at the hospital. One night, I woke up suddenly, with a feeling that I needed to go the hospital in the morning. Looking back I know it was the Holy Spirit's prompting. Mike had slipped into a coma, but I was miraculously allowed into the intensive care unit to see him.

As I touched his hand and began speaking quietly into his ear, I told him that I understood if he couldn't respond, but that the Lord had sent me here to bring him the words of eternal life. He squeezed my hand when I asked if he wanted to hear.

Simply and clearly, I explained the gospel and Jesus' love for him. When I gave him the opportunity to receive Jesus as His Savior, he squeezed my hand, yes, that he would pray along with me to receive forgiveness of his sins and eternal life. It was truly a supernatural experience! Tears streamed down my face, as I thought of Mike having a new resurrection body in heaven.

Mike died that evening, and in the following months, I began spending much more time with Helen, who had also become bitter. She eventually started going to church with me, and her heart began to thaw. One Sunday, sitting beside me in church, Helen heard the gospel explained, followed by a prayer of invitation. She elbowed me in the ribs and said out loud, "I did it! I invited Him in!"

All around the world, and in our own family, neighborhood, school and workplace, people are waiting for someone to "be Jesus with skin on." One day very soon, our Bridegroom will appear to take us forever to His eternal kingdom.

Like Mike and Helen were finally able to understand, all of our temporary trials and light afflictions will disappear at the sight of His appearance. Though outwardly we are wasting away, inwardly we are being renewed and transformed into His likeness, with ever increasing glory (2 Corinthians 3:18, 4:17-18).

Even as my precious mother's outward body wastes away with Alzheimer's, as a Bride of Jesus she is safely kept by Him in preparation for her eternal glory, where every tear will be wiped away, no more death, mourning, crying or pain (Revelation 21:4).

My dear, beloved leader and friend, Bill Bright, founder

of Campus Crusade for Christ, went home to meet King Jesus face to face on July 19, 2003, after a long battle with pulmonary fibrosis. I had the privilege of seeing him one last time in his condominium, and the radiant look on his face showed that he knew the reality of heaven awaiting him and he expressed a joyful anticipation (Heb. 12:2-24) at meeting Jesus, the One who had captured his heart and directed his every step.

A few months before he died, Bill shared about his journey through enduring the disease. "It's an exciting journey as I am preparing to meet my Lord in heaven for that great eternal wedding banquet," he said. "And in the process, people often ask me, 'How can we pray for you?' assuming that I'll ask them to pray that I will be healed. And my response is always, 'Pray that I will never leave my first love for the Lord—Father, Son and Holy Spirit, my love for Jesus.' Because as you see if you analyze the Scripture, the most important thing any of us can do is to love God with all of our hearts, with all of our souls, with all of our minds."

For now, we wait and anticipate our reunion with precious loved ones such as Bill Bright who have gone before us, their brief stay on earth over, but their legacy lives on in our hearts and in eternity. As part of this beautiful bridal host we now can behold Jesus as He trains and prepares us for our eternal rule and reign with Him as well.

The new heavens and new earth will come down out of heaven, "prepared as a Bride, beautifully dressed for her husband" (Revelation 21:2). What glory and majesty awaits the royal Bride of Jesus Christ when she is finally united with her beloved Bridegroom forever and ever. "Behold, I am coming soon! My reward is with me, and I will give to everyone according to what he has done" (Revelation 22:12).

As the Bride waits expectantly for her Bridegroom, there will be a day of His glorious return. Let your heart rejoice at His soon return. Are you ready to meet your Bridegroom King? Are you eagerly awaiting His return? "Now there is in store for me the crown of righteousness, which the Lord, the righteous Judge, will award me on that day – and not only to me, but also to all who have longed for his appearing" (2 Timothy 4:8).

No, this isn't a fairy tale, but a true eternal love story born in eternity. Let the dance of the King and Queen for all eternity begin!

As you revel in fresh revelation of His glory and majesty, I invite you to imagine what our eternal honeymoon might be like as you meditate on the "Kiss of Grace," an interpretation of our future destiny.

KISS OF GRACE—ETERNAL HONEYMOON

With the kiss of grace He awakened you from your sleep of spiritual death. He swept you off your feet and is now carrying you toward the eternal honeymoon home He has prepared for you (see John 14:2-3). Having already conquered death and hell, nothing stands in His way. Nothing will deter Him from His mission.

The marriage feast has been prepared. The table has been set. You stand in the corridor of time at the place where the door of eternity is about to swing open to receive you. Just beyond the door is singing. It is a great multitude of wedding guests who have anxiously awaited your arrival. As you soon step across the boundary from time into eternity, you will hear their song:

Hallelujah! For the Lord our God, the Almighty reigns! Let us rejoice and be glad and give the glory to Him, for the marriage of the Lamb has come and His bride has made herself ready (Revelation 19:6-7).

In that moment, all the cares of the earth-life will have disappeared. You will turn, look into the eyes of the One who set His heart on you an eternity ago. He will look deeply into your eyes with a penetrating gaze and gently whisper your name. With a heart flooded by His love, you can only speak a single word. But that one word will embody the essence of all that exists in time and eternity. With tears of joy and a realization that everything is complete, you will simply whisper, "Jesus...oh Jesus!"

Dear Father,

I eagerly await that day when this earth-life will be over and I see You face to face. Your love for me overwhelms me. You really do love me more than I could ever imagine! May I grow in my understanding of Your love. You are precious to me. I give myself completely to You from this point and throughout eternity. I do love You so much.

❧ *Personal Reflection* ❧

- Will you be ready when Christ returns? What changes do you need to make?
- Do you think about heaven often? How does it change your daily attitude?
- Do you see the urgency to reach others for Christ? What holds you back?

♛ *Crown Jewel: Hebrews 13:20*

"May the God of peace, who through the blood of the eternal covenant brought back from the dead our Lord Jesus, that great Shepherd of the sheep, equip you with everything good for doing His will, and may He work in us what is pleasing to Him, through Jesus Christ, to whom be glory for ever and ever. Amen."

Epilogue

Celebrating the Wedding

"Then the angel said to me, 'Write: "Blessed are those who are invited to the wedding supper of the Lamb!"'
And he added, 'These are the true words of God.'"

Revelation 19:9

I could hardly believe I was about to celebrate my jubilee birthday (the big 5-0)! I had been learning about "the year of jubilee" in Israel's history, and how God commanded them to "...sound the trumpet throughout your land. Consecrate the fiftieth year and proclaim liberty throughout the land to all its inhabitants. It shall be a jubilee for you..." (Leviticus 25:9-10). This wasn't just another year; it was to mark a new season of blessing and favor. Impressed with the significance of this year in my life and future, I began to think about how the Lord and I would celebrate. He had done so much in my life, and I wanted something special to honor Him.

One morning, while spending time with Jesus in the prayer garden at Canaan in the Desert in Phoenix, I asked Him, "What should we do to celebrate my Jubilee birthday?" I've learned to wait in expectation and listen for His response.

In moments, a wild response came into my mind, *Let's have a wedding!*

What, Lord? Was that You or my imagination? I prayed.

The familiar voice came again, *Let's have a royal wedding in honor of the King of Kings.*

I smiled and laughed out loud at this amazing idea, realizing that I had often said jokingly to the Lord that I relished having Him as my one and only Bridegroom, but I surely did miss not having a wedding and honeymoon! And this would be the perfect symbol to illustrate God's love for His Church, the Bride of Christ.

Then I started to doubt. I must have sounded like Sarah in the Bible, when God told her she would have a child at 90 years of age. After all, this was a crazy idea, right?

How can this happen, Lord? I prayed. He reminded me that He was the King, and He would oversee His banquet.

But how will I explain this? I thought. What will people think? Will they understand? Especially my Dad?

As I pondered this unique and personal encounter with my Lord, He overcame my questions with anticipation of the incredible privilege of honoring my King. Thus began a faith-filled dream coming true.

The next time I was home in St. Louis, I decided to tell my Dad about my dream of a royal wedding banquet. With my heart pounding, I said, "Dad, the Lord has been speaking to me."

"Oh no, what now?" he chided. I had been on so many wild adventures to foreign countries, and though he had learned to entrust me to the Lord's care, he still cringed whenever I presented my latest mission.

"Well, sit down," I said. "You know, I'm having a 50th birthday, and the Lord has given me a vision of having a royal wedding banquet in honor of the King of Kings." I paused, wondering what his response would be.

"Well," he said with surprise and humor, "I was planning a party for you, but this wasn't exactly what I had in mind." Then with a cute twinkle in his eye he added, "And how is the King going to pay for His royal banquet? Is He going to drop a piece of gold from His streets in heaven and have it fall in my pocketbook?"

We had a good laugh, and then I replied, "Dad, it's the King's Banquet and He has assured me He will provide."

My first confirmation occurred when I presented the idea to some friends I had met at Canaan in the Desert. They eagerly embraced my dream, seeing it was a "God-sized" vision, and that it could truly glorify Him.

Then my dear friend Lisa called unexpectedly to tell me she wanted to be my wedding coordinator. The Lord had chosen the perfect creative servant for the role. Lisa and I watched as the Lord began to unfold every detail of the ceremony.

Not only did He provide a gorgeous royal blue and purple banquet hall ornately decorated in gold, but the dear owner of Royale Orleans, a hotel in St. Louis, gave us two rooms adjoined with a lavish feast for a small dinner cost per guest.

Wearing white as a bride took on new meaning for me as I saw the purity it signified. On the final day, the Bride of Christ will be without spot or wrinkle. All her sins will be removed. The garments prepared for us will be woven with the good deeds we faithfully accomplish in partnership with Him while here on earth. "For we are His workmanship created for good works which He prepared for us to do before He even created us" (Ephesians 2:10).

My cousin Susan and I set out on the most delightful shopping trip I've ever had. Since I was representing Jesus' bride – and He provides our "heavenly wedding dress" – I prayed and asked Him to choose one for me.

To begin with, He had provided a gift from friends to pay for my dress. Expectantly, we went to the store knowing that we would recognize the right one. When I saw a beautiful tealength, creamy white, silky dress with flowing sleeves, embroidered work and two delicate silver heart clasps, I knew this was the one. And the price was discounted to be within my gift certificate amount!

"Well," Susan said, "you have to have glass slippers!"

I smiled, "Yes, to walk on the streets of gold!"

As we went to the shoe department, I met a sweet 17-yearold clerk named Victoria. She found the perfect translucent slippers with white rhinestones and elegant clear heels.

"Victoria," I said, "I'm having a wedding!"

"Really, how exciting!" she responded.

"It's not just any wedding," I began, and explained how I'd come to know Jesus personally and how this was a symbolic picture of our eternal destiny if we know Jesus.

I could see from her puzzled look, that this was all new to her. I asked if she wanted me to explain to her how she could know Jesus too. She said, "Yes," and as I related the amazing beautiful love story of the gospel, she expressed her desire to receive the gift of God's love and forgiveness for herself.

I could hardly believe how vacant the shoe department was at that time. It was as if Jesus secluded us for this divine invitation to be given to Victoria. As I invited her to pray with me—to say "Yes" to Jesus—she agreed. There in the quiet shoe store, she prayed with me to begin an eternal relationship with Jesus, now to be her Bridegroom as well.

I was so excited I invited her to my wedding banquet. Although she had to work and could not attend, I sent a card thanking her for her help and included a booklet on how to grow in her new relationship with Jesus, encouraging her to find a good church.

On an airplane flight I met Jeri, a wedding cake designer, and as I told her about my upcoming celebration, she offered to make a cake. We designed a one-of-a-kind cake. A royal crown was the top tier decorated with the Star of David and gold trim. The middle tier had roses and lilies with "I am my beloved's and He is mine" (Song of Songs 2:16) written on it. The final tier showed two hearts joined together, and said, "His banner over me is love" (Song of Songs 2:4). Jeri would not accept any money for her beautiful creation for our Bridegroom.

Nine hundred friends, relatives and a variety of guests were invited. The invitations had gone out based on Matthew 22. With this backdrop, I wanted as many people as possible to come to the King's banquet, and experience a foretaste of His ultimate wedding banquet, which has already been prepared.

The morning of my wedding celebration I awoke to loud peals of thunder. As I sat up in bed, I immediately thought of Revelation 19:6-7, "Then I heard what sounded like a great multitude, like the roar of rushing waters and like loud peals of thunder, shouting: 'Hallelujah! For our Lord God Almighty reigns. Let us rejoice and be glad and give Him glory! For the wedding of the Lamb has come, and His bride has made herself ready.'"

At the ceremony majestic banners, all proclaiming various names of God, made a breathtaking backdrop. But everything in the room drew the eye toward a royal throne. It glistened in gold. And at its side was a communion table set with two gold chalices.

Since Jesus was not visibly present, behind the throne we hung the blue and white Star of David with a bright flame coming out of it. In front of the table we placed a gorgeous display of lilies, in honor of Jesus, the Lily of the Valley.

The guests had arrived. The harpist had ceased her hymns. A glorious triumphal march began with the song, "Who is this King of Glory?" Dressed in royal colors, my 12 bridesmaids regally walked and danced down the aisle carrying a golden scepter and majestic crown to place on His throne, followed by banners, flags and tambourines to celebrate our King of Glory. The processional finished with the women poised before His throne--in adoration and holy silence.

My heart was beating so fast. The Lord was giving me so many hints of what our heavenly marriage feast will be like. And this was just a tiny glimpse into our eternal destiny as His Bride.

Then came the entrance of the bride as the song began, "We bow down, we lay our crowns, at the feet of Jesus...." My father escorted me, and I carried a majestic golden crown. My eyes were fixed on the shining throne mounted on gold cloth, decorated with jewels with a banner representing King Jesus on the wall behind. I proceeded toward the throne. All heaven must have been rejoicing with me, because I've never experienced such bliss and joy. My heart was pounding and my eyes were filled with tears as I humbly knelt before the throne. "Holy, Holy, Holy" was reverently played on the violin as we were silent before our King. I lay down my crown as we continued worshipping Jesus.

The presence of the Lord was there; His pleasure and joy enveloped us.

As I took my seat, along with my bridesmaids, Pastor Steve Cohen—a Messianic Jew, came up to welcome our guests and explain some of the Jewish symbolism.

Under the huppah, or traditional Hebrew wedding canopy, my father read a delightful poem about his love for me and giving me to the Lord. Symbolizing my covenant with Jesus, I shared a "Tribute to Jesus, My Bridegroom," followed by a season of incredible worship, beginning with one of my favorites: "Light of the World."

> …You're altogether lovely
> Altogether worthy
> Altogether wonderful to me
> King of all days
> Oh so highly exalted
> Glorious in Heaven above
> Humbly You came to the earth You created
> All for love's sake became poor.

Then Don Lawton, my long-time friend, evangelist and pastor, gave a compelling explanation of Matthew 22. He described everyone's dilemma in being invited to the wedding feast of the Lamb, without the means to get there on our own:

"How do you get to attend the feast?" he asked. "First, you must be invited. And secondly, you must know the Groom, Jesus Christ. The bride is the Church. The preparations were done by the Father, God Almighty. The Holy Spirit is the One who gives us the invitation by calling us, and Jesus has paid for it with His life.

"He is like no other King. He is given this title and a name above every name, because of what He did. Every knee will bow before Him, and every tongue will confess that Jesus Christ is Lord.

"Who wouldn't want to be at the heavenly banquet with God Almighty? But the problem is, we're poor, He's rich. We're dirty, He's pure white. We're corrupt, He's holy. How could we ever be invited to His glorious banquet?

"We have to be washed clean by the blood of Jesus Christ. His sacrifice on the cross for you can make you clean and pure before God. Then, when you have received Jesus as your Savior, you will see that He is also your King. And when you serve the King, you will come to love Him. And then the Holy Spirit of God gives you the invitation to come."

Representing the Bride of Christ, I gave the Divine Invitation: "I am honored that you have responded to my invitation to come today, but more than I, the King is inviting You to His banquet table. It's a divine invitation born in eternity, when God created us for His pleasure and glory." I then led a prayer to receive Jesus as Savior and Lord.

One of the highlights was a special videotaped message from Bill Bright. He began by giving me a tender, personalized Jubilee message. Knowing he would soon meet Jesus face to face, he delivered a powerful message about preparing to meet the King, and ended by praying for me and all of my guests.

My friend Pastor Greg Smith invited everyone to pray over me as I began my Jubilee year, and Pastor Steve Cohen pronounced the traditional wedding blessing over the Bride and Groom in Hebrew, followed by the blowing of the shofar, signifying the beginning of the special year.

Celebration, singing, dancing and rejoicing followed as I was honored by all my guests. Toasts were given, along with beautiful, touching tributes by my beloved friends and family. It was truly an awesome experience.

God has something special prepared for each of us, in this life and the next. On May 7, 2003, my guests and I experienced a foretaste of our eternal wedding feast. My prayer is that you also will begin to experience the great journey God has for you as you trust Him. I shared this poem at my wedding celebration, and I pray that Jesus will use it to kindle your fresh passionate love for Him.

A Tribute to Jesus, My Bridegroom

My Jesus, my life, my love,
Beloved of Your Father and mine;
Sent from eternal realms above,
Your radiance will forever shine.

My passionate Lover of my soul,
I'm captivated by Your grace.
You delivered me and made me whole,
I live to seek Your face.

My Bright and Morning Star,
You are the Fairest of 10,000 to me,
Your presence and power never far,
Awesome and amazing, altogether lovely!

My Shepherd and King,
My Champion and Cherished One.
To You all honor I bring,
After You alone I eagerly run.

My Husband and Maker,
The Lord Almighty is Your name.
The Holy One is my Redeemer,
God of all the earth is Your fame.

My heart is stirred by a noble theme,
You are my Prince of Glory.
Majestic, victorious King whom I esteem,
Creator of our eternal love story.

My precious Lamb seated on Your throne,
My life I humbly consecrate.
Your covenant love's been shown
For You, my Bridegroom I wait . . . anticipate!

One day face to face we'll meet,
My Sovereign Lord You'll be my song
As I bow down and lay my crown at Your feet,
Joined by Your wedding throng!

"Hallelujah! For our Lord God Almighty reigns.
Let us rejoice and be glad and give Him glory!
For the Wedding of the Lamb has come,
And His bride has made herself ready."

Your beloved Bride,
Nancy

NW
~ Jubilee Celebration, May 4, 2003 ~

Consider

An Intimate Love Song to the Nations

WORSHIP CD

Produced by Steve Bell

Track 1 **Shofar (Tekiah)**
Shofar played by Scott Kluge
The Eternal Love Story
Written and read by Nancy Wilson
Keyboards – Steve Bell
Psalm 45:1-2
Read by Gill Denyer

Track 2 **O Come O King**
Written by James Nesbit
Recorded at Kruta Studios
Vocals – James Nesbit, Alpha & Omega Christian
Fellowship Worship Team, Ron
Habermehl, Debi Habermehl,
Erin Crumb, Pam Walters
Guitars – Larry Raymer, Ron Habermehl
Keyboards – Larry Raymer, Georgia Habermehl
Violin – Terry Hartman
Drums – James Nesbit

Track 3 **Rest My Child**
Written and read by Nancy Wilson
Psalm 45:3-5
Read by Gill Denyer

Track 4   **Ride Savior Ride**
Written by James Nesbit
Recorded at Kruta Studios
Vocals – James Nesbit, Jim Kruta
Guitars – John Staden
Keyboards – Jim Kruta
Bass Guitar – John Krumm
Drums – James Nesbit

Track 5   **The Names of God**
Written by James Nesbit and Steve Bell
Keyboards – Steve Bell
Vocals – James Nesbit
Brian Wing	*(Hebrew)*
Cynthia Perez	*(Spanish)*
Brad Hopp	*(Russian)*
Hyang Sook Kim	*(Korean)*
George Mamboleo	*(Swahili)*

Psalm 45:5-6
Read by Gill Denyer

Track 6   **Shofar (Shevarim)**
Shofar played by Scott Kluge
My King of Glory
Written and read by Nancy Wilson

Track 7   **Jesus Heals**
Written by James Nesbit
Recorded at Kruta Studios
Vocals – James Nesbit, Donald Douglas, Pam
Walters, Erin Krumm
Guitar – Larry Cortner

Track 8   **My Suffering Savior**
Written and read by Nancy Wilson

Track 9   **Sweet Song from Heaven**
Written by James Nesbit
Vocals – James Nesbit, Cindy Perez. Steve Bell
Guitar – Dan Lee
Psalm 45:7-8
Read by Gill Denyer

Track 10   **My Bridegroom**
Written and read by Nancy Wilson
Psalm 45:9
Read by Gill Denyer
Shofar (Teruah)
Shofar played by Scott Kluge

Track 11   **Lord, I Want To See You**
Written by James Nesbit
Recorded at Kruta Stusios
Vocals – James Nesbit and the Alpha & Omega
Christian Fellowship Worship Team (Ron Habermehl, Debi Habermehl, Erin Crumb, Pam Walters, Larry Raymer)
Guitars and keyboards – Larry Raymer
Drums – James Nesbit

Track 12   **The Throne Room**
Written by James Nesbit
Keyboards – Steve Bell
Violin – Samuel Lawton
Vocals – Brian Wing, Brad Hopp, Chuck Oakley, Hyang Sook Kim, Dan Lee, Ivan Vinogradov, James Nesbit, Nancy Wilson, Marcia Meyer, George Mamboleo

Track 13 **I'm So in Love**
Written by James Nesbit
Recorded at Kruta Studios
Guitar and vocals – Ryan Aurand
Psalm 45:10-11
Read by Dela Adadevoh

Track 14 **O My Beloved**
Written by James Nesbit
Vocals – James Nesbit
Keyboards – Steve Bell
Overwhelmed with Love (The Bride's Response)
Written and read by Nancy Wilson
Psalm 45:13-14
Read by Dela Adadevoh

Track 15 **O Sweet Communion**
Written by James Nesbit
Vocals – James Nesbit, Cindy Perez, Steve Bell
Guitar – Dan Lee

Track 16 **Excerpts from "Royal Robes"**
Written and read by Nancy Wilson
Psalm 45:16-17
Read by Dela Adadevoh

Track 17 **Commissioning: Isaiah 60:1-3**
Read by Dela Adadevoh
Response: Isaiah 61:1-3
Read by Nancy Wilson
Declaration: Isaiah 62:3-5
Read by Dela Adadevoh

Track 18   Shofar (Tekiah Gadola)
Shofar played by Scott Kluge
Return of the King
Words by Molly Lawton
Recorded and arranged by Don Lawton
Vocals – Holly McDaniel
Keyboards – Don Lawton

Track 19   Revelation 19:6-7
Read by Nancy Wilson
**The Lord Jesus, the Spirit, and the Bride
Say, "Come"**

Track 20   Great is Thy Faithfulness *(In honor of Dr. Bill Bright)*
Violin – Brandon Page
Piano – David Petrie

*Additional background incidental music provided courtesy of Heart
Sounds International and Chuck Oakley.*

Poems for Further Reflection

Chamber of My Heart

My heart is stirred for You my King,
My soul within me does sing;
I recite verses of praise to Thee,
Into eternal realms I see
Gazing at Arundel Castle,
Illuminated in sunlit dazzle
What a foresight of eternal reign,
That beckons me from earthly pain;
My King in glory awaits me,
Enthralled by my beauty;
Bowing down I honor You,
Mighty, righteous and true;
Exalted among the nations,
Ruling all generations;
All glorious in wedding array,
Your grace and glory in display;
Led to you with joy and gladness,
Not a trace of sadness
I'll enter Your palace forever,
To be separated never;
For You are my fortress,
I am Yours to possess;
Majestic, loving King of all,
At Your beautiful feet I fall;
Holy, holy, holy and pure,
My passionate love secure;
In Your majesty, ride forth in victory.

NW
~ Arundel Castle, England, April 9, 2001 ~

The Dance of Grace and Beauty

A sense of wonder and delight,
As many gaze upon this sight;

The King in all His splendor,
One whom multitudes adore;

With His Beloved Bride
Dancing close to His side;

Overwhelmed with ecstasy,
Into His eyes she does see

Her own image reflected,
Never again to be neglected;

His regal glory illuminates,
Royal radiance captivates;

All heaven stands in wonder,
Loud peals of flashing thunder

Announcing the wedding day,
Eternal romance on display.
(May all saints rejoice today!)

NW
~ April 25, 2004, Cocoa Beach, FL ~

The Return of King Jesus

(Rev. 19:11-16)

I saw heaven open wide,
And before me was the King,
Faithful and True is His name,
Which the heavenly host doth sing.
Jesus sits on a horse of white,
Prepared and ready to ride,
He will judge and make holy war,
From Him no soul can hide.

His eyes are like a blazing fire,
Many crowns are on His head;
His robe is dipped in precious blood,
Angelic armies He led.

A name is written on His robe,
That He alone does know,
His name is also, "Word of God,"
By this believers grow.

The heavenly armies followed Him,
Dressed in linen white,
Ready for battle upon white steeds,
The victory is now in sight.

From the mouth of our great King
We see a very sharp sword,
The victory's sure, the battle's quick,
The world will know He's Lord!

When all are brought before the King,
All heads and knees will bow,
"King of Kings and Lord of Lords,"
Shout kings and peasants now.

NW
~ Given to Molly Lawton on December 22, 2003 ~

Beholding Jesus

Here in this holy place,
I come to seek Your face;
Broken, bruised and weak,
I hear "Blessed are the meek;"
Gazing up at Your glory
Reveals the true story;
John, in the Spirit heard
A loud voice that stirred;
Like a trumpet sound
Turning his eyes he found
Among the seven lampstands
Someone like a son of man
Dressed in a robe to His feet,
Golden sash to complete;
His head and hair woolen white,
What a glorious awesome sight!
Oh! Eyes like blazing fire,
Enflame my heart with desire;
Feet like bronze glowing,
His glory and power showing;
Rushing waters, like His voice,
Immersing my human choice;
I'm drawn to His right hand,
That is the place I will stand;
Seven stars does He hold,
Pure and radiant as gold;
Out of His mouth comes a sword!
(His name is the Word of God)
Sharp, double-edged is His Word!
His face was like the sun,
I fell at His feet undone!
In brilliant radiance He shown,
And further made Himself known;
Placing His right hand on me,

He spoke so tenderly;
Do not be afraid! It is I!
...The First, the Last, was His cry!
I was dead, but now alive forever,
Death and Hades cannot sever;
I am the Living One for you,
I've come to make all things new!

NW
~ By the river of delight, Colorado, July 6, 2003 ~

Fountain of Life

(based on Psalm 36)
Your love reaches to the heavens so high,
Your faithfulness beyond the sky;
How priceless is Your love unfailing,
Peaceful as these little boats sailing;
Both kings and poor shall find
Your heart is pure and kind;
They feast on Your supply.
Answering their humble cry
You give from Your river of delights,
Overflowing with incredible sights;
With You is the fountain of life,
Cleansing free from all strife;
In Your light, we see light,
Gazing on such a marvelous sight!
Amazing love so divine,
With You I choose to dine!
All my love and adoration,

NW
~ At the Louvre in Paris, April 21, 2005 ~

Castle at Sundown

Powder blue skies with wisps of white,
Begin to give way to coming night;
Mountains form a silhouette,
Where earth and sky have met;
A castle perched upon a hill
Beckons my heart "Be still."
My King is preparing a place,
Filled with glory and grace;
Soon the sun will disappear
And the Bright Morning Star appear
Suddenly
Bells ring out,
He will come with a shout!

NW
~ At Werdenberg Castle in Buchs, Switzerland, August 25, 2003 ~

Consuming Love of My King

Creator of all beauty,
Full of regal majesty;
My soul resonates,
Entering Your gates;
I marvel in Your presence,
Pure and holy essence;
You bid me nearer,
I see as in a mirror;
Your glory so stunning,
I come running
To fall at Your feet
With tears we meet;
Holy, Holy, Holy I cry
To my Exalted King on High;
Gentle power reaches,
Incense and prayer beseeches;
Your love overwhelms me,
'Til only Jesus, I see!

~ NW ~

A Great-full Generation

Oh Lord, we're joined with You,
Who came to make things new!
Your heart shown on the cross,
Our hearts break at Your loss;
Soon You revealed Your glory
In the Resurrection story;
You now summon us by name
To declare Your victorious fame!
Great are You Lord of all,
Empower us to give the call;
One generation shall declare,
No! to bondage and despair;
"Do not be afraid, I am here!
Come My children, draw near!"
Fear of the Lord, I will teach,
This generation we will reach!
They will tell of Your deeds,
As we sow spiritual seeds!

NW
~ November 14, 2003 ~

Set Apart for You

I came to You alone,
From my Father's throne;
Walked a single state,
Without an earthly mate;
My longing was for you,
And those My Father drew;
You are my precious Bride,
Always with Me, abide;
When you feel alone,
Your heart may groan,
But let your spirit soar
To the One you adore.
I desire your devotion,
Amidst life's commotion;
Will you passionately pursue,

And daily say, "I do?"
How precious is this gift to me,
To be set apart solely for Thee;
Master, Lord, Lover and Friend,
To You alone I will attend;
Your will is my command,
Beautifully and perfectly planned;
I rejoice and delight in You,
My only love so true.
Every day my longing grows,
I pray the world knows;
My Redeemer, Prince and King—
Creator of Everything;
"His mouth is sweetness itself;
He is altogether lovely.
This is my lover, this is my friend,
O daughters of Jerusalem."

NW
~ December 21, 2002 ~

Secret Place

Oh the beauty of Your presence,
You are all of life's essence;
Creation declares Your beauty,
Open my eyes to see
Kisses of love everywhere,
Demonstrations of Your care;
Holy Spirit, You are my seal,
Jesus' love I feel so real;
Overtake and consume me,
Ravish my heart to see;
Ignite the flame to burn,
Make my heart yearn;

More of You is my cry,
I need You to draw nigh;
Fresh revelation is my plea,
More of You, less of me;
You are my secret place,
As I gaze at Your holy face.

NW
~ July 12, 2003, On the Sabbath in Colorado ~

Royal Robes

Such royal privilege is mine,
For my Holy King to incline
His attention and affection on me,
Dressed in royal robes to see
The beauty of His righteousness,
Adorned in grace and holiness;
I approach my Beloved King,
Nothing of my own I bring;
His inner court is sanctified,
His Bride has been purified;
There's protocol in His palace,
Not any sin or malice;
The King is seated on His throne,
His majesty and beauty shone;
Beheld by eyes like fire,
Pleasing Him was my desire;
Humbly in His presence I stand,
Gold scepter in His hand;
Extended to me, He asks,
What is your request?

NW ~ March 12, 2004, Chiang Mai, Thailand ~

Listen, My Lover

Listen, my Lover!
Look, here He comes
Leaping across the mountains,
Bounding over the hills.
Song of Solomon 2:8
Your sweet presence is everywhere,
My senses are keenly aware;
The gentle breeze whispers You're near,
Bounding over the hills, You appear;
What beauty and strength You possess,
Coming to romance and refresh;
Your fragrant love envelopes me,
Opening my heart to fully see;
Jesus, Lover of my soul,
In You alone I'm whole.
I'm reminded of my childhood,
You have been so good . . .
To give me my heart's delight,
Ravishing me with this sight;
Majestic, intricate designer,
Holy, faithful refiner;
Wrap me tighter in Your embrace,
Abiding in Your holy place.

NW
~ August 22, 2003, Switzerland ~

Eager Anticipation

My heart beats with expectancy,
More of You I want to see;
Visions of Your beauty and majesty,
As You reveal Yourself to me:
King of Creation, I wait,

With reverent awe, anticipate;
You will hear my tender voice,
Cherishing You as my choice;
All for You I freely give,
For Your pleasure I live;
Desire of the nations come,
All blessing flows from
Your heart of grace and glory,
Writes every intimate love story;
A long song to the earth
You and I will birth!

NW
~ August 17, 2004, Arrival in Hawaii ~

Whom Have I?

Today my heart is lonely,
Being a one and only;
So many truths I know,
You're helping me to grow;
"Don't hide your sadness,
Wait for My gladness;
"Pain can pave a path to Me,
Embracing intimacy;"
Jesus, You are near,
My yearnings You hear;
Promised me to never leave,
Once again I choose to cleave
Betrothed, forever to You
In covenant love so true;
My flesh and heart may fail,
But Your strength will avail;
Everyday my Portion,
A refuge to where I run;
Earth has nothing I desire,
Your passion set me on fire;

You alone are my all,
Telling Your deeds my call!
Securely held by Your right hand,
Abiding triumphantly I boldly stand;
In Your gracious glory,
This is my marvelous love story!
Your Beloved Bride,
Nancy

NW
~ May 30, 2004, Orlando, Florida ~

Fresh Intimacy

Oh, what ecstasy is mine,
At Your invitation to dine;
"Come away My beloved to Me,
New depths of My love to see;"
I've chosen this day to gaze
At Your beautiful heart ablaze;
Yes, Lord, my heart's first desire
Is to burn like a blazing fire;
Your passion ignites a mighty flame
That drives me to proclaim Your fame;
My Lover is radiant and pure,
He holds the world's cure;
No one can compare,
Nor will I choose to share;
My heart belongs to my Lover, my Friend,
I bring each broken heart to Him to mend;
Covenant love so sweet,
Jesus draws me to meet;
Intimacy is enhanced,
With my King, I have danced!

NW
~ July 31, 2004, Sugar Creek Park, St. Louis, Mo., Lord's Day ~

Waiting Whispers

What delight is this glorious sight;
As I meditate in Your Word,
A piercing two-edged sword.
You have spoken to my heart,
Your will no one can thwart;
"Let all the earth be silent,
To hear Your Sovereign intent;"
The babbling brook does speak,
Peace and tranquility to seek.
Abiding in Your law,
Was when Habakkuk saw;
Wait for Your revelation,
Bringing a fresh visitation;
The righteous live by faith,
Knowing, "Thus saith!"
The earth will be filled,
All violence and evil stilled;
Knowledge of the Lord's glory
Is the climax of our story;
But now we wait in lowliness,
Fear You, Lord, in holiness;
I will rejoice in my King,
Joyful praises to You, I sing;
You are my strength and song,
For whom my soul does long;
Take me to Your heights,
Past all earthly sights;
Reveal Your Majesty,
Fierce and intimately.

NW
~ Park in Indy, November 5, 2001 ~

Rest, My Daughter

In the arms of my Beloved, I rest . . .
He has provided the very best;
For His presence is fullness of joy and pleasure,
He alone is my supreme treasure!
In the secret place I wait,
He stirs my heart to anticipate;
In communion with my King,
He makes my lips sing;
In listening to His desire,
He sets my heart on fire;
In meditating on His grace,
He reveals His lovely face;
In awe and adoration I bow,
He smiles and speaks to me now;

NW
~ August 19, 2003, Castle in Switzerland ~

Daughter of the King

(Zeph. 3:14-17)
Sing, O Daughter of Zion,
No more tears or crying;
Be glad and rejoice aloud!
The Son shines through the cloud;
He takes away your punishment,
Salvation replaces judgment,
The King of Israel is with you,
Everything is brand new!
Never again to fear any harm,
Gone is needless alarm;
On that day they will say,
Jerusalem, rejoice and pray!
The Lord God is mighty to save,

For you His life He gave;
In you He takes great delight,
What a marvelous sight;
His love quietly bringing,
He rejoices over you with singing!
Oh Daughter, can you see?
You are completely free!

NW
~ May 4, 2004, Anniversary of Jubilee (in the air) ~

My Lover, My Friend

My Lover is outstanding,
His very presence commanding,
Head of purest gold,
Limitless power untold;
Yet His lips drip with myrrh,
Like lilies, tender to stir,
His mouth is sweetness,
For my brokenness;
He tells me I'm His own,
Gracious kindness shown;
"My dove, my perfect One,
The work has been done."
You are beautiful and unique,
Free of Satan's critique;
"I belong to my lover,
and His desire is for me."
Song of Sol. 7:10
He is my Lover and Friend,
To Him I eagerly attend;
Song of Sol. 5-7

NW
~ December 30, 2003 ~

King Of Creation

All beauty emanates from You,
Grand designs so fresh and new;
Every day is a work of art,
Today the beginning of a new start;
Canvas of my life is clean,
So Your glory can be seen;
The script awaits Your cue,
My part is alongside You!

NW

Your Name

Jesus, full of truth and grace,
I look into Your face;

Yes, my Prince of Peace,
You cause anxiety to cease;

The government is on You alone,
Your glory has been shone;

There is no other name
I desire to proclaim;

Salvation is found in no other,
Please save my brother;

So many remain lost
In spite of Your great cost;

Your power is what I need
To boldly plant the seed;

Anoint me with boldness,
Protect me from coldness;

So I will fearlessly declare,
And take the time to share

The name above every name,
Full of beauty and regal fame;

Light of the World are You,
Messiah and Savior too!

Grip me with fresh zeal
To persuasively appeal…

"Come to Jesus Christ today,
He is the only way!"

I love you my Jesus
Your Bride,
Nancy

NW
~ Flying with Jesus back to Orlando, January 7, 2002 ~

My King of Glory

One so pure and holy
Became poor and lowly;
Kneeling to give assent
To the season He was sent;
Agonizing drops of blood
Opened up salvation's flood;
Purchased with such a price,
Payment made will suffice;
His beloved bride was bought
Through the costly battle fought;
Passionate love poured out
Covers all shame and doubt;
Leads me to adore,
Compelled to give Him more;
Waiting with eager anticipation,
Filled with joyful expectation;
My royal King of glory
Will complete His story.

NW
February 24, 2004
~ Written at Canaan in the desert-prayer garden ~

Queen's Canyon

King Jesus took my hand
To show me where to stand.
Look up, the path is steep,
And some waters are deep,
But I will be your guide,
Always at your side.
You asked to see My glory,
This is a glimpse of My story.
I am A to Z and in between,
No eye has ever seen.
Your seeking heart draws Me,
I'll open your eyes to see.
Winding paths keep you close,
Since I am the One who knows.
Stay near the river
Even if it's a sliver.
At times it gushes and flows,
Always My power it shows.
I'll show you the Water of Life,
Free from striving or strife,
Flowing from My Holy throne
Where all My glory is shown.
I am the Bright and Morning Star,
My coming is not far.
Proclaim, pray, praise,
Let your banner raise.
I am coming for you,
My beloved and true.

NW
~ Saturday, July 7, 2001 ~

A Temple Of Praise

Lord Jesus, I hear Your cry,
And my spirit does reply;
You are my King of Glory,
Author of every story.
All creation magnifies You,
It's what we were created to do;
Heaven is Your throne,
Where Your glory is shown;
Earth is Your footstool,
Each of us Your tool;
Where is the house You will build for me?
Where will my resting place be?
I choose the temple of Your heart,
It's been my desire from the start;
This is the one I esteem,
Not always what may seem;
He who is humble and contrite,
Is One in whom I delight;
At My word, tremble,
On your knees assemble
With a pure heart and clean hands.
This is the One who stands;
In His holy place,
Always seeking His face;
Welcoming the King of Glory
To complete His story!
The Lord almighty and strong,
My everlasting song!

NW

Consider

An Eternal Love Story

There is a love story that surpasses time and enters into eternal realms. It was created in the heart of the God and King over all the Earth.

"I will sing of the Lord's great love forever;
With my mouth I will make your faithfulness know
through all generations.
I will declare that your love stands firm forever,
That you established your faithfulness in heaven itself"
(Psalm 89:1-2).

The story starts with the creation of the world, and then it centers in a garden, the Garden of Eden. It was magnificent in beauty and diversity. All kinds of trees, pleasing to the eye and good for food, were there. God created humans in His own image, then blessed them and assigned them to multiply and manage His creation.

In the middle of the garden was the tree of the knowledge of good and evil. God told man that he was free to eat from any tree in the garden except the tree of the knowledge of good and evil.

God loved man and entrusted him with His awesome creation to enjoy. He wanted to protect and provide for them. Desiring a relationship with His beloved creation, man and woman, He gave them free will to choose.

One day the crafty serpent came to the woman and deceived her. He lied to her, telling her she would not die if she ate of the tree of the knowledge of good and evil. The serpent accused God of withholding good from them. "When the woman saw that the fruit of the tree was good for food and pleasing to the eye, and also desirable for gaining wisdom, she took some and ate it. She also gave some to her husband, who was with her, and he ate it. Then the eyes of both of them were opened, and they realized they were naked; so they sewed fig leaves together and made coverings for themselves. Then the man and his wife heard the sound of the Lord God and He was walking in the garden in the cool of the day, and they hid from the Lord God among the trees of the garden. But the Lord God called to the man, 'where are you?'" (Genesis 3:6-9).

This is the tragic entrance of shame and evil into the world. This was sin. It brought a separation from our loving Creator, who designed us for an intimate eternal relationship.

Because of God's perfect and holy character, He had to punish sin through the curse put first on the serpent, and then upon the man and woman. There would be pain in childbirth, and painful toil all the days of their lives, before man returns to the dust of the earth.

The perfect love story is marred. There is sadness and longing in the heart of man for his Creator, the One he is made by and for.

But the story has only begun, for in the heart of our God is a divine redemptive plan to rescue man from eternal death.

Throughout the pages of history a scarlet thread is woven, revealing the mystery of the ages. A foreshadowing of a coming Messiah and Savior is seen through the covenant promises given to Abraham, Isaac, Jacob. We see the Passover Lamb with the blood placed on the door points, protecting the Israelites from the plague of the killing of the first-born son.

Instructions are given to Moses to build a tabernacle where God could meet with His people to have fellowship. But they must adhere to the sacrificial system to atone for their sins before they could be accepted by God. Every part of the process pointed to the need for cleansing and atonement for sin. A perfect spotless lamb had to be offered on the Altar of Burnt offering.

Then, prophets were raised up by God to prepare His people for the coming Messiah. Isaiah told of a new beginning: "The people walking in darkness have seen a great light; on those living in the land of the shadow of death a light has dawned" (Isaiah 9:2).

The Jewish people were not expecting a suffering servant, but this is what Isaiah 53 described, one who would bear our sins and sorrows. "Surely he took up our infirmities and carried our sorrows, yet we considered him stricken by God, smitten by him, and afflicted. But he was pierced for our transgressions, he was crushed for our iniquities; the punishment that brought us peace was upon him, and by his wounds we are healed" (Isaiah 53:4-5).

Time marched forward, and the people waited, anticipating their Messiah to deliver them from Roman oppression. Little did they know that God had pre-ordained this plan of salvation before the creation of the world.

Isaiah's prophecy was fulfilled through the birth of Jesus. "For God so loved the world that he gave his one and only Son, that whoever believes in him shall not perish but have eternal life" (John 3:16).

Our loving Creator, God, sent His own Son, Jesus Christ, to be the payment for our sin. He was crucified on a cross to be the perfect sacrifice to pay for our sins. The King of glory removed His royal robes to die to take our place.

Jesus Christ is the hero of our love story. He entered human history for one purpose only, to pursue each one of us, His Beloved Bride.

Jesus came to show us the love of our Father God. He wants to restore us to an intimate, loving relationship with Him. He alone has the right to do this, because of His perfect, sinless life and His sacrificial death in our place.

He invites us to receive this amazing gift of grace, completely underserved. "For it is by grace you have been saved, through faith – and this not from yourselves it is the gift of God" (Ephesians 2:8).

God, our Father, wants to adopt us as His beloved child. "Yet to all who receive him, to those who believed in his name, he gave the right to become children of God" (John 1:12).

It is a personal invitation for every human being. God desires that we respond to His invitation. "Here I am! I stand at the door and knock. If anyone hears my voice and opens the door, I will come in and eat with him, and he with me" (Revelation 3:20). Jesus is asking, "will you be my Bride for all eternity, to reign with me eternally in my kingdom of love and truth?"

A royal wedding celebration is being prepared, and your presence is requested. "Let us rejoice and be glad and give him glory! For the wedding of the Lamb has come and his bride has made herself ready" (Revelation 19:7).

Will you be ready as His Bride, purchased by the blood of Jesus, cleansed and made ready to reign and rule with Him for all eternity? He desires to establish His throne in your heart to have an intimate relationship with you. You can respond to Him now through simply expressing your heart to Him in prayer.

"Lord Jesus, I recognize Your amazing sacrificial love for me. That you died in my place to rescue me from the penalty of my sin. I receive Your gift of forgiveness of sin and accept Your invitation to come into my heart. Make me the person You have designed me to be, and prepare me to be Your bride for all eternity! Thank You for pursuing me and introducing me to Your eternal love story!"

Our journey in this earthly life is an opportunity to grow in our intimate relationship with the One who calls us "His Beloved." His heart is so huge that it will take all eternity to know the pleasures of His love. I invite you to join me on a journey to know His heart, as we worship our Lover and King, Messiah, our eternal Bridegroom.

Consider

Opportunities for the Bride

To help support national youth workers or adopt a high school campus in Kenya, send donations to Student Venture Kenya
Account: 2788987:
Campus Crusade for Christ
P.O. Box 628222
Orlando, FL 32862-9841

To sponsor a child in Nakuru (Tumaini Children's Home)
please send donations to:
The Mission Society
P.O. Box 922637
Norcross, GA 30010-2637
Note: G.O.A. Kenya #000850 (Tumaini)
www.gloryoutreach.org

Check out www.studentventure.com to discover opportunities to minister locally and globally.

Other Resources

Destined for the Throne, Paul Billheimer (Christian Literature Crusade, 1975)

A Divine Invitation, Steve McVey (Eugene, OR: Harvest House Publishers, 2002)

The Divine Embrace, Ken Gire (Wheaton, IL: Tyndale House Publishers, Inc., 2003)

A Kiss a Day, Jamie Lash (Hagerstown, MD: EBED Publications, 1998)

FireBride, Margaret Morgan Moberly (Lake Mary, FL: Creation House, 1999)

Hawaii's Monarchy: Kings and Queens and the Royal Palace (Honolulu, HI: Aloha Graphics and Sales, 1978)

Heartcry, A Journal on Revival and Spiritual Awakening, A Quarterly of Life Action
Ministries (Buchanan, MI: Issue 30, Winter 2005)

His Majesty Requests, Rebecca Park Totilo (Enumclaw, WA: Pleasant Word, a division of WinePress Publishing, 2003)

Lover of My Soul, Alan D. Wright (Sisters, OR: Multnomah Publishers, 1998)

Make Haste My Beloved, Frances J. Roberts (Ojai, CA: King's Farspan, Inc., 1978)

My All For Him, Basilea Schlink (Minneapolis, MN: Bethany House, 1999)

Secrets of the Secret Place, Bob Sorge (Greenwood, MO: Oasis House, 2001)

Song of Songs, Watchman Nee (Fort Washington, PA: Christian Literature Crusade, 1965)

The Song of the Bride, Jeanne Guyon (Sargent, GA: The SeedSowers Publishing House)

Special thanks and honor is due

James Nesbitt, who designed the awesome cover and composed most of the worship songs on the CD. James, thank you for your godly influence and help in producing the CD. The dream would never have been realized without your sacrificial service for our King!

Kae Mentz, who has majestically illustrated the message of The King and I. What a privilege and delight to work with you to honor Him! You have been gifted "for such a time as this." I'm in awe at the gift He has bestowed on you.

Becky Hill, my final editor who was God's gift to me! I'm overjoyed at your skill and heart to communicate my message so clearly, and with such beauty! Thank you for your friendship, advice, and patience in every step of the process!

New Life Publishing, you have been so faithful to work diligently with me to bring this vision to reality! Pat Pierce, thank you for believing in me and believing God! Dave Stedman, I always knew I could call and you would be there to help! Michelle Watkins, for seeing us through to completion with your expert help!

Steve Bell, your gifted and able skill in producing the CD is deeply appreciated! I'm still marveling at how the Lord brought you along just when I needed you! Thank you for assuming the role of Producer! You are amazingly talented and a joy to work with! I have loved every minute!

Chucky Oakley, your incredible contribution of bringing your expertise and Heart Sounds International resources for indigenous worship music added so much. What a gracious friend you are!

Dan Lee, I'm continually amazed at how multi-talented you are! Thanks so much for sacrificially giving your time to help produce our worship CD.

Don, Molly, and Samuel Lawton who contributed immensely to this project and their heart to worship the King, including Molly's poem, "The Return of King Jesus" put to music, Samuel's violin instrumental, and Don's musical arrangement, preaching and godly counsel. Also thanks to David Petrie and Brandon Page, who's musical skill added so much.

Holly McDaniel, thank you for sharing your incredible voice and gift of music with us! I pray the Lord will continue to use your music greatly! You have a beautiful voice that radiates His glory!

My dear friends in Hawaii who encouraged me in writing this book and provided a place for me to write and be thoroughly inspired. Sherel Stosik, Katherine Huske, Nancy Reid and Bev Page…I'm forever grateful for your loving Aloha hospitality!

My amazing friend and administrative assistant, Sharon Peck, who typed and formatted all my manuscript and poems, as well as many more things that helped immensely. I am so wonderfully blessed through you! You are a treasured friend!

Erik Segalini, my expert consultant and friend, who gave his counsel and later in God's perfect time, provided me with an incredible editor, Becky Hill. You're the best!

Evangelical Sisters of Mary of Canaan in the Desert. Sister Rebekkah, Mother Basilea, and each one of your devotion to Jesus has so inspired me in my journey of embracing and writing about "the Bride of Christ." You have modeled it for me!

My precious Dad, Mom, and family, who have loved me and helped to bring my Jubilee vision to reality, through their prayers, support, and generous gifts! Words can't express enough of how your influence has shaped me and this message!

Lisa Thompson, my Jubilee Wedding coordinator, precious fellow missionary, and dear friend. Without you, my dream of the "Royal Wedding Banquet" would never have been fulfilled. I'm eternally grateful for you and our kindred hearts!

My 12 bridesmaids who encourage, inspire, and accompany me on this journey toward our "ultimate wedding"… Marian, Peggy, Molly, Pearl, Sandy, Jenny, Sandy, Marcia, Donna, Lisa,

Anita, and Julia, you will forever hold a special place in my heart! You are each a part of this book and CD!

Cindy Perez, George Mambeleo, Brian Wing, Brad Hopp, Hyang Sook Kim, Ivan Vinogradov, James Nesbit, Dela Adadevoh, and Marcia Meyer, the beautiful voices on the worship CD. What a joy it has been to work with you! Your gracious contribution has honored Our King and I pray it will impact nations!

Scott Kluge who prophetically blew the shofar for our worship CD with such power and skill! Thank you, Scott. Our King was honored!

Pearl and Sandy, my mentors, intercessors, and beloved friends who prayed and gave generously to see "The King and I" produced! I love you dearly! We are a cord of three knit together in Jesus, our Bridegroom.

All my beloved friends and ministry partners around the world who have supported me in prayer and generous giving to send me to the nations as the King's Ambassador. May our King reward you richly!

Gordon and Emma Korell, Gayle Anne Vanfulpen, Dr. Veronica White, Marian Drops, Don and Karen Jubel, Mary Jane Morgan, Nancie Reid, Jeff (Albert), Rainey Abbott, Beth and Tim Manor, Uncle Jim Wilson and my precious Dad who gave the initial funds to launch this project by faith! Thank you for believing with me! Karen Faith Heller and Raoul Garcia, who encouraged me all along the way. And my cousin Susan, for providing the outfit for my picture! Thanks Sue, I love you all!

There are so many more friends around the world whose names are recorded in heaven…and etched on my heart…those who prayed and believed with me for "The King and I"…I'm eternally grateful!

And most importantly, I thank our Bridegroom King, Jesus Christ, our Beloved Lord and Savior! "Now to the King eternal, immortal, invisible, the only God, be honor and glory for ever and ever. Amen" (1 Timothy 1:17). I love you Jesus!!!

❧ *About the Author* ❧

Nancy Wilson lives in Orlando, Fla. and serves her King as His ambassador to the nations. She is the Associate National Director for Student Venture and an international ambassador for Campus Crusade for Christ. Nancy has written three other books and speaks all over the world to audiences of all ages. Her passion is to proclaim Jesus, help prepare His Bride and build His Kingdom. She has various messages for conferences, retreats and outreaches. If you would like more information about Nancy's books or ministry, please visit **www.nancywilson.org**, or call (407) 826-2174.

Chosen with a Mission:
Are You Ready for the Adventure?

(with study guide)

First Love (devotional)
Romancing His Bride and
Responding As His Bride

In Pursuit of the Ideal
Finding your identity and living in true freedom

About the Illustrators

The Prophetic Art of James Nesbit

Prophetic Art is art that foretells the coming of the King and His Kingdom. It has been said, "A picture is worth a thousand words." James Nesbit, is an artist who uses the gift entrusted to him to speak to the earth with color and image of the beauty of King Jesus and His Eternal Kingdom.

We invite you to visit the on-line gallery of James Nesbit at www.preparethewaymin.com

From Kae Mentz

It has been a privilege to be invited, as an illustrator for this expression of the King's Love, by Nancy.

This King is the Only perfect, eternal ultimate One who loves unconditionally. I believe that God Himself desires to be known by each of us. His intentions and heart are completely pure and good and powerful. My life passion is to be an instrument of introducing Him as Healer of those broken places and Rescuer of our souls from destruction and death.

As a mother of four, I set artwork aside for many years while I was immersed in the full-time action of family and youth ministry. These relationships have been my greatest joy over the past 25 years.

In the maturing of our family and ministry, through the struggles and the blessings, my passion to express life through the visual arts has only grown. Since 1997 I have been able to develop this gift through studying and the coaching of some wonderful artists. These are now becoming another of the greatest adventures in my life.

A few of the adventures are described on my website (www.astillsmallVoice.net) and I would welcome ideas, interest or questions. Prints are available in all sizes, upon request (Kae.Mentz@StudentVenture.com).